I0820124

FINDING THE PUCK

FINDING THE PUCK

Leadership Lessons from My Journey Through Blind Hockey

CRAIG FITZPATRICK

Library of Congress Cataloging-in-Publication Data available upon request.

This book is available in quantity at special discounts for your group or organization. For further information, contact:

Triumph Books LLC
814 North Franklin Street
Chicago, Illinois 60610
(312) 337-0747
www.triumphbooks.com

Printed in U.S.A.
ISBN: 978-1-63727-910-6
Design by Nord Compo
Photos and graphics courtesy of Craig Fitzpatrick

CONTENTS

FOREWORD

THE GAME OF HOCKEY—perhaps more than any other sport on earth—requires a level of perseverance and humility, from the moment you step on the ice through any stage of development. Hockey has core values that were not chosen at random, but defined by the game itself, and consistently found in players throughout the generations. And for all of its traditions and nostalgia, it has always been a sport willing to change and grow—to get faster, bring people closer, and be more inclusive.

As an executive at the National Hockey League focused on growth and social impact, it is both an honor and a privilege to introduce this groundbreaking book by Craig Fitzpatrick on blind hockey and, more importantly, his perspective on the true power of the sport. The NHL has long been committed to promoting access and opportunity within the sport, ensuring that hockey is a game for everyone. While we deliver the most skilled and competitive hockey in the world each night, we understand the profound and consistent impact that the sport has on individuals, communities, and society.

My first conversation about blind hockey took place after meeting Willie O'Ree, a pioneering figure in the history of the NHL, known primarily for becoming the first Black player in the league when he was called up in 1958. Most people in hockey know basic facts about Willie. He was born in Fredericton, New Brunswick. He met his childhood hero, Jackie Robinson, only to follow in his footsteps. He played for the Boston Bruins. But what many people do not realize—and I was unaware of—is that by the time Willie O'Ree made his NHL debut, he was playing with a visual impairment.

At the age of 19, during a game in the minors, Willie was struck in the right eye with a puck. The injury resulted in him losing 95 percent of vision in that eye. Doctors advised him to stop playing hockey due to the severity of the injury. But Willie was determined to continue the pursuit of his dreams. He said to himself, *Willie, stop focusing on what you can't see, and focus on what you can see.*

Willie adapted to his condition; he developed his skills to compensate for vision loss. He (remarkably) kept his impairment a secret from coaches and teammates. But more than anything, Willie never lost his willingness to work hard, his desire to be great, or his self-belief. He used his life situation to become stronger, and tapped into a new level of resilience and perseverance. Willie has gone on to become a symbol of hockey's greatest values and attributes—and still takes the time to share his story with children today.

Like Willie, Craig shares a powerful message that delivers hope and empowerment to those in similar circumstances. This book showcases Craig's remarkable struggle, journey, and triumph. It illustrates life's possibilities when you believe in yourself and recalibrate your own idea of limitations. It demonstrates how the inputs of resilience, determination, and an unyielding positive spirit leads to the most amazing of outputs.

Some of the most interesting developments within the hockey ecosystem over the last two decades have been in the adaptations to gameplay and equipment to support growth for disabled communities. From sled to special hockey, and deaf to blind hockey, small but mighty groups formed throughout North America to build derivatives of the game that meet people where they are and allow more people to enjoy an equal measure of competition, comradery, and exhilaration from the game. Be it Hockey Hall of Famers or blind hockey players, all are connected through the game's core values. The NHL is proud to support the continued development and growth of blind hockey.

For those reading this who may be blind or have visual impairments—or have family or loved ones with this experience—I think you'll find this book not only educates and informs but inspires. At the NHL, we want you to know that you belong in hockey, that it is available to you, and that your participation in the sport—as a player, fan, employee, or in any other capacity—is valued and valuable. For some chosen few, hockey is a job. For most of us, hockey is a tool to help unlock our greatest human potential.

The NHL and I share Craig's hope that blind hockey will one day soon become a Paralympic event. I will continue to encourage NHL Clubs and athletes to work with and support the blind community as it advances this amazing sport.

Kim Davis
Senior Executive Vice President
of the National Hockey League

PROLOGUE

On October 12, 2000, I didn't have time to notice I was going blind.

Around 11:30 AM that day, I pressed my foot to the gas pedal of the pickup truck that was carrying myself and two of my Air Force colleagues, speeding us toward a headquarters tent in the midst of a hot, sandy airfield on the Arabian Peninsula. We'd received an emergency notice to report for an intelligence briefing. Less than 90 seconds after I walked into the tent, I found out that the *USS Cole*, a Navy destroyer, had been attacked off the coast of Yemen. My unit, being close in proximity to the scene, would get very busy over the coming weeks and months, helping transport supplies to Yemen and bringing more than a dozen coffins to Ramstein Air Base in Germany for their return home. I didn't know at the time that the Global War on Terrorism would start in a few years. I hadn't heard a ton about this terror network called Al-Qaeda who carried out the attack. On a more personal note, I didn't know when I'd get to go home. I did know that Al Gore and George W. Bush were in a dead heat for the upcoming presidential election; that back home my favorite sports team, the Colorado Avalanche, had just started their season; and that my next few weeks were going to be very, very busy. Throughout a nearly sleepless October and

November, a nasty combination of stress, desert sunlight, and aviation chemicals kicked off a chain reaction in my retinas that would alter the course of my life, ultimately leading to legal blindness.

I had just turned 24 years old.

I arrived back in the U.S. to my home near Travis Air Force Base, California, in February 2001. On my return, I learned that my performance leading my unit had landed me a highly sought-after position on the staff of a four-star general at Scott Air Force Base, Illinois. I loved working on the flight line as an Aircraft Maintenance Officer. I loved the fast pace. I loved the smell of JP-8 fuel as jet engines roared for take-off. And I loved leading people.

For all these reasons, the Air Force had to drag me kicking and screaming off the flight line. Once they did, I packed my bags in California and ventured out to my new duty station on exit 19A in a cornfield of Illinois, just across the Mississippi River from St. Louis, Missouri. Along the way I stopped in Denver for St. Patrick's Day, got a chance to ski for a day up in Vail, and watched my beloved Avalanche beat the Red Wings on their way to the National Hockey League's Stanley Cup playoffs.

I noticed on my drive from California to Colorado that I'd gotten sloppy as a driver. I noticed that skiing in Vail seemed much tougher this go-around than it had been when I was skiing regularly while in college less than three years earlier. I noticed I couldn't read the scoreboard at the hockey game. My mind convinced me that I had one beer too many on St Patrick's Day; that it had been a long time since I'd previously skied and Vail was a tough mountain, so I was just a less capable skier. As I drove from Colorado to St. Louis, crossing much of Kansas in the middle of the night, I had a couple near-misses behind the wheel, and my mind decided I was just tired and driving poorly.

I started my new high-pressure job, working as the youngest officer on the staff of the Commander of U.S. Transportation Command, and I decided to enroll in a master's degree program at Saint Louis University. I started classes on September 10, 2001.

The following morning, I came to work at U.S. Transportation Command headquarters, spending some of my time figuring out how I'd balance my duties for that day with my need to leave for class, across the river in St. Louis, at around 4:00 PM. When the first plane hit the Twin Towers, some of my colleagues turned on the news on a TV in the office. They asked me why I was standing so close to the TV, and I explained that I was really concerned about the story. The second plane hit, our commander was informed that America was in the midst of a terror attack, and all hell broke loose.

I spent the next several hours, from 10:00 AM to 3:50 PM, in a giant command post building, straining to see the flashing dots on a screen half the size of a city block that showed all the planes flying in America, both commercial and civilian. Blinking dots began disappearing from the board as planes landed and others did not take off. At one point during the day, the board tracking airplanes across the country went completely dark. In times when I've gotten examined by ophthalmologists—doctors who care for patients with eye conditions—allowing them to examine me in order to track the progression of my vision loss, they usually administer a test where I'm supposed to track blinking dots and press a plunger when I see one. I fail the test with flying colors every time, as I've now got less than 10 percent of vision remaining—only a thin ring around the border of my eyesight. Purely peripheral vision.

I think about the big board tracking 9/11's airplanes every time I take that test.

I made it to class the night of September 11. It was a public sector budgeting class, and Saint Louis University decided to go ahead with classes that evening as more news rolled in. I walked in an hour late, still in uniform, shaking and dejected. As I strained to see the PowerPoint slides of the professor presenting insights on how the money to fund government programs flows, it began to dawn on me that maybe I couldn't see the screen because I needed new glasses.

My eyesight continued to decline over the winter of 2001 and early 2002. I managed to balance helping Transportation Command prepare for what would become the Global War on Terrorism while commuting across the Mississippi River three nights a week, from O'Fallon, Illinois, to the campus of Saint Louis University. The chapters, charts, and classes got tougher and tougher for me to track. My average time to complete homework for each grad school class doubled, then tripled. To compensate for this, I began returning to my office at Scott Air Force Base around 10:00 PM three nights a week, studying at my work desk, and then sleeping on the couch in the break room.

In February 2002, I finally made it to the optometrist. She dilated my pupils, shined a painfully intense light onto my retinas, and looked closely. I'll never forget the sound she made when she discovered the damage that the previous eighteen untreated months had done to the backs of my eyes.

She sighed for what felt like an eternity, then said, "This, uh.... Let me go bring someone in for a second look."

Dilated, unable to see much at all, and beginning to be concerned, I heard the door close, then open again a few seconds later. A second doctor entered the room. Then a third. Each examined me in the same manner as the first, and they each saw the same things: yellowish flecks of a fatty protein, called lipofuscin, choking the life out of my retinas. These were telltale signs of an advanced version of a rare retinal condition known as Stargardt disease.

The optometrists at Scott Air Force Base referred me to Wilford Hall Medical Center, which is the Air Force's top hospital, located in San Antonio, Texas. The Air Force's top retinal specialist, Dr. Mike Jumper, delivered the news I'd been dreading: it was Stargardt disease. I was well on my way to being legally blind, if not already there. My dream of a career in the Air Force would have to come to an untimely end, a little less than four years after I'd graduated from the Academy.

I was devastated.

I returned to Scott Air Force Base the next day and told my commander about the diagnosis. I went to Saint Louis University that night and told my professors the same. I asked both work and school if I could take two weeks off to process the whole experience. For me, "process" looked like this: I sulked for a day, then called a travel agent, booked 10 days in Prague, and stayed extremely drunk for about nine and a half days.

I returned home determined to do two things: serve out my five-year commitment to the Air Force and finish my master's degree.

My commander and co-workers were amazing—they helped me file procedural appeal after procedural appeal in order to delay my medical discharge. I continued to do the best job I could for the Air Force by day, and I buckled down even harder for my studies at night. I enrolled in three summer courses to try to accelerate progress in my master's program, since I knew I was in a race against an aggressive eye disease and I had no idea how long I'd be able to do the required coursework, even with tripled-down effort and all-nighters to get through the material.

I finished my master's in Public Administration in December 2002, 15 months after I began the program. To my surprise, I finished ranked first in my graduating class, and the faculty awarded me summa cum laude honors (Latin for "with highest praise") for my master's thesis. I shifted focus to finishing my time in the Air Force as strongly as I could while interviewing for civilian jobs that I thought I could do blind. My last day serving on active duty in the military was June 3, 2003.

My experience between February 2002 and June 2003 didn't seem like a leadership lesson at the time. It seemed like some combination of a cruel joke—some sort of punishment by God, or life, or fate—combined with a string of demoralizing lessons about the difference between thriving and simply surviving. However, in the 20-plus years that have passed since this pivotal time in my life, I've realized that the absolute shit-kicking that life put on me at that time helped me gain the most important quality that all leaders have to possess: self-mastery.

Throughout this book I'll tell a series of stories about my journey as a blind man, hockey player, businessman, and husband. I've learned a lot of hard-earned lessons about leadership by continuing to challenge myself in life, in sport, in business, in friendships, and in love, and I hope those lessons help whoever takes the time to read this book. But the most important lesson I've learned is this: life will give us all tough situations, and the way we handle ourselves and see our way through them allows ourselves the space and grace to lead others. To that end—going blind, learning to play hockey, betting it all on a tech start-up—those are all versions of *Finding the Puck*.

Chapter 1

RESILIENCE

Hockey's a strange pastime for a blind person. But, in many ways, it gave me back my life.

Sunday, April 3, 2022

I'm in Pittsburgh, suited up for the deciding game of the second hockey championship I have taken part in over the past 10 days.

And I'm a wreck. Not mentally, not anymore. I'm in a much better place than I've been for the last several years. Perhaps I'm in the best place, mentally, that I've ever been.

But, boy, physically, I'm a disaster. The day before, my team squeaked out a win over a much better adversary. We had no business taking that game. They were far better than us—faster, more physical, more coherent as a team. But that's one of the fun things about hockey. A worse team will sometimes get a little lucky and pull out a victory, undeserved perhaps, but necessarily hard fought.

I feel the effects of that fight all over me, not to mention the effects of many other games. I am bruised, sore—stiff, feeling every year of my four-plus decades on this planet. In the not-too-distant past, I tore the lateral collateral ligament in my knee as well as my left meniscus. I was wearing two custom knee braces as a result. An improperly healed right fibula, shattered back in 2018 by a dirty hit, the opposing player sweeping my legs, caused me constant muscle spasms. My right ACL had popped a few years earlier during a warm-up, and I'd played the game anyway. I had been told, almost scolded, by medical professionals that I needed to get both knees replaced.

None of this made me play scared. My modus operandi consisted either of 800mg of ibuprofen or two large beers before game time. I would slap those braces on my legs and hit the ice.

The day before, during Game 2 of this best-of-three championship, I found myself as the only guy between the opponent's fast-breaking forward and our goalie, and I had to do everything possible to prevent a point-blank shot. Skating with all the frantic speed I could muster, I backchecked, taking a low angle that would—I hoped—cut their player off from my goaltender just a few feet before the net.

I wasn't fast enough though.

Almost but not quite catching the other team's speedy forward, I realized the chance of them scoring on this play had just skyrocketed. I found myself in a desperate situation and it called for a desperate decision.

I dove.

Sprawling forward, lashing out with my stick, I missed the puck but my body swept the other skater from his feet. His skates, which have blades as sharp and as long as meat cleavers, missed my neck by millimeters.

This wasn't a legal move I'd made, diving to take the other player out. It wasn't even a smart move, considering the risk to both me and my opponent. But strategically it was the right thing to do. Even though I went to the penalty box, I probably stopped a goal. My team would have a chance to beat the short-handed shift of the next two minutes. This, most coaches would say, is a preferable option to hoping, in that dangerous moment of the break-away, our goalie could make a save one-on-one.

As I sat in the penalty box for those two long minutes, questions began to cross my mind. I had nothing better to do than cheer as my teammates held off our opponent's attack. Cheer and, of course, think. *What if I had gotten hurt? What if those skate blades had cut me?* I had just married the woman of my dreams a few months earlier. We had begun trying to have a child together. I started to think of her, of this future family we wanted to enjoy, and the voice of wisdom in my mind—moving quickly from cause to effect to solution—asked me: *Why the hell are you still playing hockey, Craig Fitzpatrick?*

This question, you see, wasn't one I'd ever really contemplated before. But it was certainly a valid one for any 40-something man or woman still playing the game competitively. Hockey is a violent, young person's sport. But, in my particular case, and in the case of all those on my team and in this tournament, it contained an even deeper profundity. You see, this wasn't just any beer league tournament. This was something much more specialized and exotic: the USA Hockey Disabled Festival's Blind Hockey Championship.

Read that again.

Yep. *Blind.* Not able to see. Without vision. And *hockey.* The fast-paced, seemingly dangerous sport of hockey. Not exactly words that seem to go together. Not in the everyday world. *Blind* and *hockey.* Hmmm.

I didn't grow up playing or even watching hockey. But neither was I born blind. That began to happen a few years after I graduated from the U.S. Air Force Academy, while serving as an Air Force officer, way back in 2002.

Born in Pennsylvania, but having moved to South Carolina at the ripe old age of eight, my formative sports had been baseball, then soccer. I wasn't the most gifted athlete, but definitely the try-hard kid on every team I joined. I'd be the one running out infield grounders and sliding into first base headfirst, Pete Rose style. I pitched for a while, practicing out behind our garage at a target painted on a haybale, as if I were in a scene from a Kevin Costner or Jimmy Stewart baseball movie. I stuck with pitching until I discovered soccer. South Carolina, and especially my high school there, boasted great soccer, the best in America, which was both a blessing and a curse. I got to play with really great athletes and learn the game at a high level, appreciating its fluidity and strategy—both things that baseball seemed to lack. However, soccer didn't have much of a future for me. When it came time to make the high school team, I simply didn't have the chops to compete on what was, back then, the best prep team in America.

South Carolina has no professional teams in any of the major sports, so becoming a fan of any particular club or game wasn't really in the cards for me during my formative days. That changed in a big way, though, during my sophomore year at the Air Force Academy.

I could still see then; otherwise, I would never have been admitted to the Air Force in the first place.

I had to study a lot, as the academics at the Academy were intense.

I remember that my roommate was being noisy one night and I had a thermodynamics exam the next day, requiring some serious prep time. I needed quiet, somewhere I could be alone. And that's not an easy thing to find in any college environment.

Air Force had a hockey team, the Falcons, but they were terrible. Nowadays they're a fairly well-respected Division I college program, but back then, in 1995, they were still in Division III. With the team drawing few fans, the ice rink seemed like a place that would offer the peace and quiet I needed, even during a game, so I took my books and went to that night's contest.

It worked. The few dozen people seated around the perimeter of the rink barely made any noise in the crisp, voluminous space of the building, with its wrap-around bleachers and high ceiling. Bright lights and cold air in the rink also might help keep me awake and focused through some heavy reading, I thought. So I found a seat high up under the rafters, kicked my feet up on one of the armrests of the empty row to my front, and cracked my thermodynamics primer open on my lap.

The game flowed on below me.

I read—and tried to memorize—rules for heat flowing from a warmer area to a colder one, and the first period ran its course.

I read about the imperfect conversion of heat into work, and noticed that ice hockey seemed to embody some of the same rules and flow as soccer, but with much more speed and grace.

I then heard a great crash, far below me in the rink, as two players collided into the boards. Definitely not a soccer move. And, more to my fascination, both players got up and continued on about their business, chasing the little disc of vulcanized rubber around the rink. In soccer, if any sort of contact like that happened, the whole play would stop. One of the players, or both of them, would have been clutching their legs, arms, necks or backs, trying to draw a yellow card. Yet that wasn't the case here. Play continued. These were tough dudes in a tough game.

I put down my book and allowed myself to watch a little more.

Air Force won that game.

I remember the players high-fiving, celebrating with whoops as they left the ice, their movements less graceful as their skate blades chonked across the solid floor of the tunnel toward what I supposed must be a locker room hidden under the stands. Less graceful, but still fascinating—filled with testosterone, different from any other sport I'd seen. I could hear their individual voices on the way back to their lockers, because only about 10 people remained in the building to cheer on the team.

I forgot my thermodynamics book up beneath the topmost row of the stands and had to come back later for it. But that wasn't all I came back for. I started to watch the games as often as I could.

Fast forward to 2012.

I had been overseas, working in Dubai (more on that later). I'd also gotten married in 2011 and my return to the United States, taking a job with Booz Allen Hamilton, making plenty of money for my new wife and me to be comfortable, seemed like the dream scenario. I even bought a house. But I had also started drinking pretty heavily, two or three nights a week, working 18-hour days, sleeping in my office in Arlington, outside D.C. I was putting a ton of pressure on myself because I'd promised my wife's parents, when asking for her hand, that I would support her through her MBA at Georgetown as a condition of our marriage. This wasn't a great dynamic. My wife, Brita, didn't handle graduate school very well, sequestering herself in a room upstairs that we'd walled off as her "office"—meaning that she and I lived almost independent of each other, sharing a house more like friends who sometimes hooked up than like an actual supportive married couple.

But having given my word to Brita's parents, I immersed myself in the Booz Allen consulting work. However, only a year after I started, I became one of the casualties of a huge management restructure and was let go.

But I had to make ends meet. I was the only one earning a paycheck in our new little family.

I took on a bunch of meaningless contract work, writing proposals for a small company outside of D.C. With almost no vision, it proved to be maddening work.

I was living almost alone, much of my time spent in my own head, so much so that I went to a local branch of the Department of Veterans Affairs and requested an appointment with a therapist, coming away from one of the first sessions with a diagnosis of depression and a solid dosing of Wellbutrin. God, what a terrible thing that was for me, making me jittery, increasing my sleeplessness. The therapist insisted I continue the drugs, adding in a sleeping pill, which to me seemed like the stupidest idea: give a depressed guy who is drinking to cope with his life a prescription for sleeping pills!

I plodded on until I could go no further. I needed to feel like I controlled something in my life. I needed to feel like something in my life was mine and mine alone.

This proved to be an important crossroads for me. I faced a decision to wallow in my pain, to turn toward blaming my disability for the situation I'd found myself in, or to do something about it. I wanted to do something. Desperately, I wanted that. But what? What could that something be?

Skating.

I don't know how the thought came to the forefront of my mind.

It had been there in the background long enough.

But right then, at that moment, it bubbled to the front.

Brita and I signed up together, Sunday morning classes, level one, basic skating as offered not through some local hockey program but through U.S. Figure Skating. Sunday mornings were perfect for me: it would give me a reason to temper my drinking on Saturday nights. I invited Brita out of a mistaken belief that learning to skate together would help us reconnect. She lasted all of four or five lessons, then went back to her solitary study room. But she was there with me in the beginning, the two of us taking our first wobbly steps together.

Our lesson was held in the middle of a public skating session with several dozen other skaters, all of them coming and going at their own paces, tracking snow and shavings of ice from the rink onto the rubberized mats so that everything effervesced with a wet, clean smell.

The instructor met us off the ice, had us lace up our skates, and walked us around on our unfamiliar new footwear, tried to show us things like how to fall forward, catching ourselves with our hands, rather than backward in order to avoid smashing in our brains. Of course, I couldn't see much of what the instructor demonstrated. I kept trying to look down to see my feet, but I couldn't. I couldn't see them when I had tightened the laces either. My vision, at that distance and angle, left me with a black hole. I'd tightened them poorly, using my sense of feel alone.

After perhaps 10 minutes, the instructor led us out onto the ice.

I managed to keep upright for a few short steps as Brita and I held hands. We made it a few uncomfortable creaking tiptoes out toward the middle of the ice, where other skaters zoomed past us, enjoying the freedom of the open ice session. Brita had a lot of fear and a sense of caution about the whole thing. So I was put into the position, again, of supporting her. But eventually, on my wrongly sized, wrongly laced, wobbly plasticized rental skates, I struck off on my own with all the enthusiasm of the hockey superfan I'd long since become. This was my dream, my moment.

And, boom, down I went.

Bruised from my left hip to under my arm.

I got up. Tried again. And down I went. This continued for the whole of the lesson, but it must not have been too unordinary, as the instructor never put a halt to my self-destructive enthusiasm.

My body went mostly purple over the next few hours after the lesson, and I could barely walk for several days, but I went back to the session the next week, and the week after that. I didn't tell my instructor that I was blind until after the third session. If he was surprised, he didn't say so, but the disaster of my first few attempts at skating now made more sense to him.

My goal of these first skating lessons, as I mentioned, mostly involved finding something, anything, that would lift me from my depression. A secondary benefit, I thought, would be to give Brita and myself an experience over which we could bond.

Brita gave up, though, after just a few sessions.

I did not.

And, in fact, a new goal started to form in my mind: I wanted to play hockey.

Blind hockey.

Even I hadn't heard of it.

It existed, though.

Using a hollow puck, about double the size of a normal hockey puck and made of welded sheet metal filled with ball bearings, it makes noise as it caroms around the rink. Any stick that hits it gives off a clank. As it slides over the ice, those same small ruts and ridges and abnormalities of slickness and grit on the frozen surface make the ball bearings inside the puck jangle.

The reactions of blind players are different, sometimes slower, sometimes more hesitant, but often more subtle as well. Percent of blindness factors into that, but so too do many other faculties—not just a player's ability to use other senses but also level of training, familiarity with teammates, creativity. Much of the game, as I've described above, is powered by senses other than sight.

I went all in.

For the next 10 years, as I worked my way out of not only the menial jobs I'd taken on to support Brita but also out of the relationship with Brita altogether, hockey really became my salvation, the thing that got me up in the morning, kept me going, and gave me a reason to keep working on myself.

It's a strange pastime for a blind person.

But, in many ways, it gave me back my life.

Chapter 2

TOUGHNESS

For every challenge that comes with being disabled,
there's an opportunity to live a good and full life
or use self-doubt and self-pity as a reason not to try.

MY FATHER, JOE FITZPATRICK, was a tough son of a bitch. And, of course, growing up under the influence of such a personality is almost always a double-edged sword. Toughness gets ingrained in everything you do. But expressions of love must often be earned the hard way too.

I was born in Dad's hometown—in the vicinity of a Rust Belt relic called Shamokin, in Pennsylvania, which flourished during the era of coal mining industrialism. We didn't live in Shamokin itself but over the hill from it, in a farming town called Sunbury. We had a coal furnace in our old farmhouse, and I learned to shovel the messy lumps when I was four years old. Truthfully, I liked it. The process of shoveling contained an element of play, the same sort that a kid with a toy tractor might undertake in a sandbox, only my labor produced a real result.

Dad had served as a corpsman—which is the term for a medic—in the Navy. He was attached to a Marine unit, fast-roping out of Hueys into the jungles of Vietnam to patch up injured Marines. I never got to know him as a man, but I think we would have liked each other. I hope so.

My first real memory of him is from when I was about five years old, out on that farm in Sunbury. I was trying to fly a kite, running toward a hill that led down to where my mom tended a half-acre kitchen garden, very necessary to supplement our groceries. On the way down the hillside, I tripped over a tree root, fell headlong, and landed on top of my left arm, which got wedged under a rock. I broke both the ulna and radius. My father, who was on a tractor at the time, heard me scream over the noise of plowing. He jumped off the rig without shutting down the engine and came running to where I writhed on the ground, my kite tangled around me. When he reached me, he told me to squeeze his fingers with my left hand. I couldn't. My left hand refused to make a fist. Dad scooped me up, threw me into the front seat of his car, and sped off for the hospital. I remember the sense of quiet he exuded during the drive, though he looked over at me a few minutes after we'd left our long gravel driveway and asked how I was doing.

I said, "It hurts, Dad."

He took his eyes off the road to focus on me before answering, "Don't tell me it hurts. It's just uncomfortable. You'll be fine."

I replay that clip often in my head. It's one of the few pieces of wisdom that have stuck with me from the interactions I remember with him.

Dad really wanted me to be a pitcher in baseball. He himself had played first base. I was small for my age and, to make matters worse, I'd also already skipped a grade, making me both small and a year younger than my classmates. Certainly, I did not cut the figure of the stereotypical physically gifted kid who would take the mound on a baseball team. Still, my dad started down this road with me right from the earliest days of baseball practice. During coach-pitch and even T-ball, he'd have me stand beside the mound. Back home, we'd spend what seemed, in my young mind, hours and hours trying to get my tiny four fingers to grip the seams of the baseball. Back behind the barn he'd squat down with his first baseman's mitt, stomach protruding between his white T-shirt and his dirty jeans, a cigarette hanging from his mouth, making me throw him pitch after pitch to work on placement.

Out in this same yard in Pennsylvania, one day he set up a target for me to throw at, for when he couldn't be there—a box filled with hay upon the face of which he painted a target. I remember Dad just standing off in the distance watching me pitch against this target one day. When I'd finished a set of 10 balls, and hit the target with all 10, I started to pick them up and put them back in the bucket for another round. Dad came over then, patted me on the head, and said, "Good job." I could hit the target with all 10 balls pretty regularly, but I usually choked when he was watching. This ended up being one of the few times I remember succeeding under his gaze.

I didn't get a lot of compliments from that man, but I remember that one clearly.

He was probably thinking, at that time, *God, this scrawny little kid isn't ever going to amount to much of an athlete.* He knew I was a smarter than average boy, but I knew already that I amounted to a poor excuse for an athlete.

Looking back on it from my vantage point all these years later, perhaps his message and his plan wasn't so much to make that little boy a world-class athlete but instead, to teach me something more important, a lesson about work ethic and how, even with the most rudimentary of tools, practice and perseverance can make all the difference. Now I'm the opposite: I play my best hockey, and perform my best at work and in life, when the pressure is on—an enduring trait that I first learned under Joe Fitzpatrick's gaze.

The last day of school before Christmas break in the fifth grade—December 19, 1986—I had just turned 10 years old. By that time we had moved to Irmo, South Carolina, abandoning Rust Belt Pennsylvania. My passion for sports had shifted to soccer, but my dad still made me play baseball, and I'd also started doing Cub Scouts. The previous night we'd all gone to my Cub Scout holiday banquet and stopped at Kroger on the way home to get donuts for the following morning. At around 10:00 PM, my dad put me to bed and told me he loved me. Those were the last words he ever said to me.

Walking back from school with my brother Brendan at about 3:30 PM that day, I remember talking about what we hoped to get for Christmas. Of course by then I knew Santa Claus wasn't real, but Brendan still believed, and I knew I'd be putting together Castle Grayskull, the He-Man headquarters toy palace he'd been asking for all year, for him. Brendan was six years old and in kindergarten but even in my exalted position as a fifth-grade older brother, I secretly felt excited to play with Castle Grayskull too.

When we reached the bottom of Rusty Barn Road, the street we'd moved to in Irmo, I saw our mom waiting there. The end of our driveway was 200 yards uphill from the house, quite a climb up that road, so it was unusual to see her there. She'd never waited for us at the driveway's end any other day.

This spot is ingrained in my mind for many reasons: it's where I'd wait with my siblings to catch the school bus; it's the spot where I got beat up by a school bully when I insulted him for being dumb (which he was) and bad at soccer (which he was not); and, most importantly, on this particular day, it was the spot where Mom met us and ushered us in silence down the long hill of our driveway that fateful day. She told us she needed to talk to us, and she held us by the shoulders, crying softly, as we walked those 200 yards. The junction of Rusty Barn Road has never been a happy spot for me since then.

We reached the house, went inside, struggled through the hallway and living room to our parents' bedroom, where she sat down on the edge of the bed, facing us—me 10 years old, Brendan six—while little Conor, just two years old, sat bewildered beside her at the foot of the bed.

I don't exactly remember the words Mom used to tell us Dad was dead.

What I do remember is that Conor spent the next six months asking when our dad would be coming home. It broke my heart every time I heard it.

I also remember my mind going to another place as we rode in the limousine that followed the hearse containing my father's ashes. In this moment, the sounds I heard were those of my mom trying to muffle her tears and my siblings fidgeting around. I'd never been in a limousine before. I played with the power windows, which I'd never seen before either, just to give my fingers something to do. But my mind detached, going to a still and somber place where pain couldn't touch me, almost as if I was replaying that one line of advice from my father: *Don't tell me it hurts. It's just uncomfortable. You'll be fine.*

This moment is the first time I remember sending my mind out of my body to escape pain. But I've gone to this place often in the years since then. It's the same place I sent my thoughts when going through basic training at the

Air Force Academy, or trying to push my body through a third period of a hockey game, or pulling an all-nighter to finish a tough technology sprint. It's the same place I sent my mind for more than a year after my eye doctor told me I was losing my vision and would be medically discharged from the Air Force. Some people say that when you're tough it's because you are able to face fear and pain head-on and push through it. That's never been the case with me. I get scared and feel pain, but losing my dad at this early age in my life taught me the skill of ignoring fear and pain long enough to accomplish the task at hand.

Whenever my mind snaps back from this far-off somber place, the transition usually comes accompanied with another emotion: rage.

After my father's funeral, I spent an anger-fueled four years in school. Though I continued to pull A's in all my schoolwork, I acted out in countless ways, butting heads with teachers, mouthing-off to coaches, and generally acting out all my anger at any authority figure in my life. Once, I chased a babysitter out of our house with a hatchet when she hit my youngest brother, Conor, for drawing on the wall with a crayon. He was four years old at the time. I was 12. (Hopefully, the statute of limitations for attempted murder for minors has expired by now and it's okay to admit to this!) I don't think I really would have hatcheted the babysitter, but I certainly thought about it when I heard Conor crying.

Teamwork, perhaps a sense of belonging, finally overcame this period of sullen rage. As my undersized body failed to elevate me in sports, my mind compensated.

I made our high school science team, and we won the South Carolina State Science Olympiad my freshman year. The teamwork high I got from a mentally focused pursuit struck me as equally satisfying as the same situation in sports. Perhaps it was even better because I was able to excel at it in a way that I couldn't physically in sports. Mental competition felt like a sport to me, and I came home with the same sort of gold medals and trophies. By this moment in my life, I already realized I wasn't going to make it as a professional athlete. Our school excelled at sports. We were the best in South Carolina in soccer, near the top in any number of other sports too. So only the biggest and most physically advanced kids got to enjoy being part of those teams. By studying angles and structural engineering, I won a gold medal for building the lightest and sturdiest balsa wood bridge that supported the most weight. I baked the wood to remove water weight and was able to have my five-ounce structure support more than 80 pounds. My bridge kicked the shit out of every other high school team in the state of South Carolina, including those with seniors doing calculus, and its victory put our team over the top to win the championship. It also allowed me to achieve the same rewards of belonging, group flow, and recognition that other young men found on our high school sports fields.

That little breakthrough, winning with teammates, allowed me to stop resenting school. I realized I could get a lot of satisfaction out of academic accomplishment and that teamwork applied equally in school as it did in sports. I also realized that, while I could use brute force to lever my way through most academic challenges, as classes got harder, a cooperative team approach became not only more fulfilling but also kept me more engaged and eased my workload.

The trick I had learned, first going to a quiet place in my mind, then emerging into a state of rage fueled by the loss of my father, helped me punch above my weight academically and physically. It could have impaired me if the violence of that rage got out of hand, but instead I learned to use it to my advantage.

Continuing on the soccer field even as I turned part of my focus to academics, I learned to provoke this intensity as early as possible in games. This led to some pretty goals, lots of slide tackles, and a love-hate relationship with every coach under whom I played. I was a scrawny, undersized, not-very-talented kid who used grit and aggression to be selected for classic soccer in my early teen age group. If I'd not been the oldest kid of a single parent who opened checks in the mail from Uncle Sam every month, maybe I could have pursued soccer longer. Maybe, if I still had a father, I would have been able to afford the attempt at soccer success as the least talented but "try-hard" kid in one of the most competitive soccer areas in the country. Instead, at age 15, I hung up my cleats and got a job bagging groceries at a Harris Teeter grocery store so I could afford gas to get myself and my siblings to and from school in the $800 car my mom had scraped the cash together to buy.

What shaped me even more than dealing with my own issues was suddenly, without preparation or any roadmap how to do so, being thrust into the role of coach and quasi-parent to my siblings.

I became the family math tutor because Mom had been an English major. Math wasn't her forte. I always breezed through multiplication and division, but it came with difficulty to the other kids in our family. As a result, I had to teach myself how to teach math, not just how to do it. I re-read my math books and learned not only the concepts but also the process of teaching. I also came to understand, early on, that different people learn in different ways, since each of my siblings approached math in different ways. For instance, I taught one sibling how to multiply three times five by dumping out a box of cereal on the table in piles of five, then picking three piles of five and asking how many pieces of Cracklin' Oat Bran that totaled. This sibling needed to see the piles, whereas my other siblings were more comfortable just with the numbers on a sheet of paper. My siblings' brains worked differently from one another. And that was okay. The lesson it taught me, to value and work within others' capabilities, stuck with me all through my life and has helped me succeed as a coach, in blind hockey and in business environments alike.

I read to Conor every night as well. At age 12, and eight years his senior, the books I read weren't ones that would normally interest a four-year-old. He got a lot of history at an early age and, as a result, developed a love for it—eventually taking a history degree from the University of South Carolina.

When Conor was six, I helped coach his soccer team, basically filling in the role of volunteer dad. I figured out pretty quickly that Conor was more athletic than most of his teammates, but I also had to explain to him that being a good player didn't mean having the ball all the time. Learning to pass and help on defense counted much more in terms of overall team success. Those aren't really things that most 14-year-olds are lecturing younger brothers about or working through verbally, even if they're figuring it out themselves.

As a result, I both learned the game better for myself and learned empathy for my own teammates.

The most difficult lesson Conor had to learn while playing soccer was that he really had to work at skills he wasn't good at, and he had to do so repetitively, developing and committing to a work ethic. He was naturally good at both soccer and baseball. If he had the same work ethic as me he would have gone pro, no doubt in my mind. As catcher, even in the Little Leagues, he could throw out a runner from his knees at second base without standing up. But he never internalized a commitment to improving his weaknesses in the same way I did.

Another skill I learned at this time: cooking.

With Mom working and Dad leaving nothing in terms of a will, we went through some pretty lean times. Mom did well enough. She's been employed by the University of Michigan Institute of Social Research since 1978. Still, the necessary extra hours she put in at this job meant that, while she cooked good meals most nights, there were also plenty of times she had to work late and either I cooked dinner or we kids ate cereal. I learned not only to cook for survival but also for enjoyment, finding reward in developing those skills while also knowing I was taking care of my siblings. This "work" supporting my brothers transfers now to something I like and find joy in with regard to team sports: being the first one to arrive in the locker room, the last one out, making sure my teammates have what they need to succeed. It's a trauma response, left over from this time of scarcity in my childhood, but it's the sort of positive traumatic growth that should be recognized for the good it does.

I don't know if I'd be a very good person if it wasn't for my brother Brendan. My youngest brother, Conor, grew up to become a strong adult, well-adjusted after all this. He doesn't need much from anyone. But going all the way back to these days when I became something of a surrogate father for all of my siblings—I think my soft spot for people who need my help comes from my middle brother. Richard Brendan Fitzpatrick was born May 21, 1980—the day *The Empire Strikes Back* came out—and he was born with two-and-a-half strikes against him. He's deaf in one ear, 40 percent deaf in the other, has facial deformities that took more than 10 surgeries to correct, and was born with a separated esophagus. He wasn't supposed to live long, and he ate from a feeding tube until well after he could talk. When Dad died, I think it became pretty clear to me that Brendan needed me to be there for him. The feeling I get when I spend time with Brendan is similar to the feeling I get when I step on the ice with a blind athlete. I'm a deeply flawed person, and at times I can be an asshole—but I learned to be my best self because I had a brother who was born different, and I loved spending time with him. I see a lot of him in the toughness and gratitude that I see in blind athletes.

Now, not all my familial responses to my father's death were positive. I developed some resentment toward my siblings exactly because they needed my help. It's tough, in the mind of a preteen, to embrace the idea that your siblings need help simply because they're younger. In my inner voice I asked the question *Why me?* a lot. Having to overcome that voice, to answer that question, helped me mature and made me a more patient coach in later years.

I also dealt with a feeling of being "ripped off" for not getting to play sports like a normal kid after my dad died. This likely contributed to the passion with which, later as an adult when I had time and means, I dove headfirst into blind hockey and carried on until I made Team USA. There, the combination of caring for my teammates, harnessing a sense of blind rage to push myself, and being able to absorb pain, helped me channel my limited—and by that time visually impaired—physical abilities into athletic performance.

My dad smoked like a chimney. He was overweight. He died of a heart attack. This affected me, in all the ways mentioned above, but it also affected my mom.

She was actually the talented athlete of the family, earning money in college as a tennis pro. She can throw a tight spiral with a football and—when my father died early—she stopped smoking and became a fitness instructor, choosing to teach classes because she couldn't afford to pay for them. She kept this up for over 20 years.

To this day, the smell of smoking revolts me. When my dad died, I used to dip my mom's cigarettes in toilet water, break them in half, whatever I needed to do to get her to quit. She kept hiding them and I kept hunting them down and then messing them up, until she got the message. This isn't a typical relationship between a 12-year-old and his mom. The thought, as a young boy, that my heart might suddenly explode in my chest, as it had done for my father, also wasn't a normal idea.

My mom's been a great fan of my sports. She's in the stands all the time, coming to see me play blind hockey around the country. But she hasn't always been the best student of the sport. (If I offered her a million dollars to explain the concept of icing, for instance, she'd go home penniless.) But she's been my cheering section.

This uncommon relationship with my mom, and with parenting in general, manifested in one other notable way during my high school years: my relationship with girls.

Because I was the child of a single mother and the oldest male in her brood, I didn't know how to have a flirtatious relationship with a woman. I didn't get to watch a dad or older brother or uncle demonstrate how to interact in that way. My senior prom date had to ask me to prom. A lot of my anger and drive, my wanting to do well in sports and school, grew from the idea of hoping, somewhere in a heaven I barely understood, my dad might be watching and feel proud of me. Unlike other boys my age, I wasn't competing in athletics or in school to impress the ladies as much as I was trying to send a message of perseverance and love to my missing father.

When I put on the Team USA jersey for the first time, about to step onto the ice for the first-ever international competition, playing Team Canada, I could hear my mom in the stands, her normal conversational voice over the sea of people in the stands as the national anthem played. I love that she got to see that moment. I just hoped that, from wherever he was, my dad was watching too.

Chapter 3

LEARNING THE RULES

I had to get over my fear of looking like an idiot really quickly.

ICE HOCKEY ISN'T THE EASIEST GAME for a novice to learn. Blind hockey only complicates things further.

For regulation hockey, even learning the game to the level of following it as a fan means you must understand a number of funky rules that aren't present in most other sports: icing, offside, a variety of penalties from spearing (which is poking someone with the stick) to checking (which is legal as long as you do it correctly) to the rules around a player touching the puck with his or her hands (hint: you're allowed to catch it and drop it but not pass it, throw it, or slide it to another player with the hand). Oh, and the puck. That bad boy is significantly different from most other objects with which sports are played. A one-inch thick, three-inch diameter bullet of vulcanized rubber weighing about six ounces, the puck is fast, hard, usually black, and can be a devil to see on the ice for even those who have the full use of their sense of sight.

Then, when a person decides to jump from just learning the basics of hockey as a fan—which was my level of involvement in the sport from the moment I first discovered it during that search for studying solitude at the Air Force Academy—to actually participating in hockey as a player, a whole additional set of skills must be learned and applied.

Skating, for one.

Instead of solid ground, the inventors of ice hockey put this particular aspect of the game right in the name: *ice*. Slippery ice. A sheet of smooth and flat whiteness, recently shaved and watered to make it even more diabolically slick. And, to boot, rather than a flat-bottomed shoe with normal surface area to prop a player up, someone decided to venture out onto the treacherous playing surface trusting their balance to nothing more than two knives strapped to the bottom of very stiff leather boots.

A new player's ankles revolt against this. They wobble. They collapse. They chafe where the boot grips the foot, at least until the player puts in the time to build up their muscles and get their feet accustomed to having so much control exerted through the ankles.

Unlike a knife, which has one edge, the blade of an ice skate has two—an inside edge and an outside edge, both sharp enough to shave with and between which the process of skate sharpening (which is a regular requirement) creates a small concavity for the whole length of the blade. The existence of two edges allows a player to lean to one side or the other and cut into the ice. The blade also has a bit of gentle, almost unnoticeable curvature from toe to heel, which facilitates a skater's ability to turn by allowing them to rock forward or backward, shifting the center of balance ever so slightly. For the novice, for the person taking their first few hesitant steps on the rink, learning to work these edges to create propulsion and stability is anything but easy. Stepping flat on the ice, as most beginning skaters tend to do, doesn't bring the edges into play very much. Likewise, skating slowly also under-utilizes these unique features; a skater cannot cut or turn hard until moving relatively quickly, leveraging the physics of bodyweight and centrifugal force to drive the sharp edges into the ice. So there's a gap, a chasm a skater must experience and overcome, through trial and error. And this skill can't be learned from a book! Only after a new skater develops some basic ability to move on the ice can they advance toward mastering other unique hockey skills such as the handling of a stick; the catching and sending of a pass; the proper and comfortable wearing of equipment; the various ways of shooting; or, beyond the mere physical skills, the mental aspects of figuring out how and when to apply all of hockey's weird rules.

I undertook this initial learning process by signing up for a learn-to-play-hockey program at a rink in Rockville, Maryland. This was early in the winter of 2013, when my first marriage was already on the way down the tube. Rockville, for a guy like me without the ability to self-drive, proved anything but an easy commute. The trip from my house to the rink took one hour and 50 minutes each way on public transit, and I had to learn to balance my hockey gear on my back in a backpack, holding my sticks like jousting lances, while riding the mile from my home on Capitol Hill to the Union Station metro. I tried to find a learn-to-play-hockey program inside the D.C. beltway, but all the leagues required at least some level of skating proficiency (which I'd been working on) and also hockey experience (of which I had none).

D.C., ever since about 2006, had been immersed in what I call the "Ovechkin Effect." The arrival and spectacular play of Alex Ovechkin for the Washington Capitals NHL team drove a humongous upswell of interest in the game, both for spectators and for those who wanted to learn to play. The Capitals were looking to start a learn-to-play program for adults, but it hadn't been launched at the time I decided to take up the sport. D.C. also brings together itinerant folks from all over the country because of the way the nation's political and military apparatuses center there. The benefit to hockey is that people who grew up in the north, in Minnesota and Maine and Massachusetts and Michigan, end up being drawn into the community, even if only sometimes temporarily. They form a basis for pretty decent beer league hockey. But this pool of players just doesn't allow for a total newbie, like me, to latch onto a team.

Thus, I needed to get myself to Rockville. With my wife unwilling and uninterested in supporting me by driving several times a week into the Maryland burbs, I found a friend, Andy Ashcroft, who also happened to want to learn hockey. Even better, he was fully sighted and could drive. We joined a group of about 20 others who signed up for the Rockville rink's learn-to-play class, all of us adults, 18 or so men but also two women. (Interestingly, only one of the women was really there for hockey's sake. The other wore a nice little scarf under her equipment, for some added flair, and bathed herself in perfume before taking the ice. She had come to meet dudes.)

The eight-week-long program included fundamentals like stick handling and skating refinement and also a primer on how to apply the rules of the game. I'd watched plenty of hockey by this time, mostly sitting a foot from a TV screen and yelling in the general direction of pixelated skaters. I now, quickly, learned how much tougher obeying the rules while also skating could prove to be—the offside rule especially.

For a typical player, let alone someone who can barely skate and barely see, it's tough to pay attention as the blue line whizzes by under you. It's buried beneath the ice. Its blue color varies according to how much, and how carefully, the rink's crew painted it, as well as whether it has ever melted or scraped away. Most blind players have too poor vision to see a colored line buried under a couple inches of ice; to further complicate things, many legally blind athletes have color vision issues as well. On top of that, the glare from the rink's lighting, usually banks of cheap fluorescents, can create a shine over the blue that appears blindingly white. Moving fast; trying to coordinate blades, stick, legs, arms; trying to watch for the puck; calling out to your teammates to let them know where you are—all that makes the sinister, sneaky presence of that blue line much tougher to anticipate than it seems when watching professional players from the Colorado Avalanche gracefully attack and regroup, attack and regroup, with the blue line somehow nearly always where they expect. I've probably gone offside more than 1,000 times, and I'm one of the more conscientious players when it comes to position. Most blind hockey players have to do one of three things: count strides to remember position; use sound in relation to the bench or areas of the ice to know roughly where the blue line might be; or follow the flow of play and just pray we're on the correct side of the line. It's a wonder blind hockey games aren't stopped every 30 seconds for offside violations, but somehow we figure it out.

Perhaps I should back up and explain the concept of offside a bit more. For those who don't know hockey well, it's necessary to mention that a sheet of regulation ice for hockey is divided by three fat lines painted beneath the middle section of the clear ice, as well as two thinner lines on either end. One of these fat lines is the center line. It's usually red, and it divides the rink into two halves. The other two fat lines are blue. They denote each team's defensive zone. The two thin lines on the far ends of each zone, way down by the goals, don't factor into the offside rule, but instead demarcate another rule called icing.

When an offside violation occurs, it is because a player (or sometimes several players) on the attacking team have crossed the blue line of the defending team before the puck. In blind hockey, By not allowing an attacking player in the defending zone, this rule prevents a team from stationing a player on the far end of the ice to receive a long Hail Mary–type pass. It also means that, frequently, when a team is attacking and has successfully crossed the defender's blue line with the puck, if that puck comes back across the blue, all attacking players must cycle out of the zone, back over that blue line, before renewing the attack.

Confusing, right?

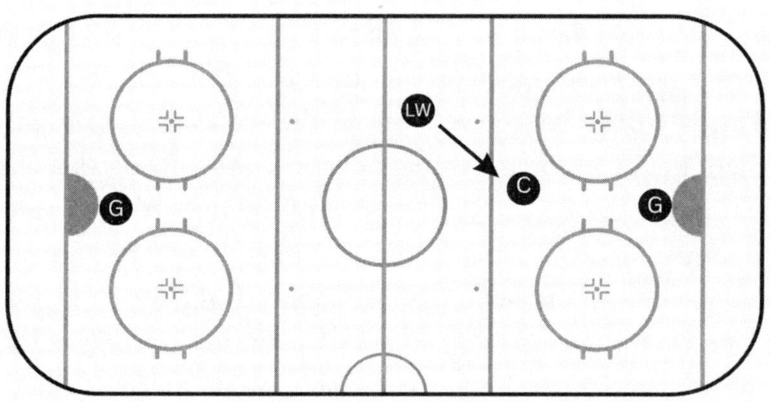

Try adding to that an almost complete inability to see the darn line. When I started lessons in Rockville, I hadn't quite yet learned to map the contours of a rink in my mind's eye. Now I know roughly how many strides it takes me to reach the blue line, the red line, the further blue line. Rinks are not all the same size, but they're generally of a similar proportion and a quick jaunt around, during warm-ups, is now usually enough for me to figure things out. I can count my strides and guesstimate how far I am from being offside. Then my technique when I feel I am near my opponent's blue line is to turn and skate crosswise about where I imagine the line to be, looking out of the one corner of my eye that has a little vision to hopefully locate the spot where the blue line is usually painted on the boards above the ice. I can't see the weak blue streak below me through the ice at all. My eyesight is almost completely gone looking down. Sometimes I can't see where the blue is marked on the boards, either. Often, especially in the beginning, I'd be hopelessly offside, and the ref would have to whistle the play dead, preventing my team from capitalizing on an attack that otherwise would have had high chances for success. I learned, after a while, that it was better to pull up three strides early and skate along parallel to the blue than go three inches across.

Not being able to see well also means I get called for many other kinds of penalties. Most beer leagues don't allow checking, but even if they do, the only person who can be checked is the puck-carrier and, even then, a skater can only take a couple strides before legitimately checking their opponent. Being blind, though, I run into people a lot. The penalty for that is called charging. Or sometimes, if less egregious, the ref might call it interference, which is getting tangled up with someone who doesn't have the puck.

The underlying emotion as I learned this new sport was frustration. I had to get over my fear of looking like an idiot really quickly. For instance, it should have been a 50-50 proposition whether I chose the right door or the wrong door when called for penalties. But it felt more like I was right 10 percent of the time and wrong the other 90 percent, ending up in the wrong penalty box (each team usually has a box assigned for their own players, to help keep them separated from one another in case of brawling); or even jumping the boards to come off the ice during a shift on the fly only to find I'd jumped onto the other team's bench. I felt like an idiot because I was learning to play around people who could see. It gave me a chip on my shoulder that really no one else understood that I was visually impaired. They probably wouldn't have cared anyway, but I was able to turn my frustration into a mental edge. Although the people I first learned to play with were sighted, they were learning alongside me, and it allowed me to feel more comfortable about making mistakes.

Obviously the game of ice hockey is well-established. Its professional leagues and Olympic status have endured for decades. For this reason, changes to the game only ever occur in incremental fashion and aren't designed to accommodate blind players.

But starting a new sport, blind hockey, resulted in a very different situation. We could and did change the rules of the regulation game in a few important ways.

Blind hockey began in Canada, with the first team, the Toronto Ice Owls, established in 1972. Between 1978 and 1979, teams in Montreal, Calgary, and Edmonton followed, with Vancouver forming a team in 1995. The team from Montreal played with a hollow apple juice can, which made a ton of noise as it awkwardly tumbled around the ice and was easily dented. The team from Toronto used a hollow, six-inch plastic BBQ wheel with piano pins inserted in it to make it rattle and give it some weight. Vancouver, Calgary, and Edmonton used a small steel puck that had been custom welded and had skate rivets inside to make it rattle. Like most everything else between the English and French parts of Canada, this conflict took a while to iron out.

In 2013, Canada held its first unified event, where players from Toronto and Montreal used the Ice Owls' BBQ wheel because it was considered a middle ground between the Vancouver puck, which was too small and moved too fast, and the Montreal can, which was too big, too slow, and not shaped like a puck. The teams competing against each other during these games started normalizing a few other rules too.

The three main adaptations they made were:

1. Requiring goalies to be completely blind. Blindness levels are established by an organization called the International Blind Sports Association (IBSA). It has created three tiers, B1 to B3, with B1 representing the most severe level of impairment. To compete as a legally blind athlete a skater must be at least B3. I'm a B2. Goalies must be B1. Blind hockey doesn't mean everyone is completely blind. It would be nothing but a car crash if everyone were. People have argued for it, or for a separate tier of blind hockey featuring only those who are completely without vision, but such a game would be accessible only for people who learned to play before going blind. To my knowledge there are only a handful of such people in the world who can skate out—i.e., not play goalie—and do anything meaningful with the puck. Related to the requirement for goalies to be rated as B1, the Toronto vs. Montreal rules mandated a change to the size of the goal net. It is a foot shorter than in regulation hockey because the puck doesn't make any noise in the air, and thus the shorter net gives a totally blind goalie a better

chance to stop the puck. They mainly tend goal by playing positionally: moving their bodies toward where they hear the puck, trying to keep their angles blocking the net.

2. The second rule has to do with the puck. Blending the Toronto and Montreal innovations, blind hockey uses a 22-gauge steel cylinder filled with eight noisy ball bearings. It's roughly double the size of a regulation puck and weighs twice as much. Because the ball bearings rattle while moving, the puck is an equalizer, allowing all players to participate in the play, no matter their level of vision. When the puck isn't moving, only someone with a bit of sight—like my ability to see out of one corner of my eye—can ever find it. Those who are B1 must use memory alone. The puck is, unfortunately, one of the biggest barriers to participation in the sport. It has to be custom manufactured, which takes a long time, and they therefore cost about $40 each. Only a few people know how to make them, and in a typical game we go through about three of them. As soon as the puck hits one of the metal goalposts, it's usually hopelessly dented. Because of this, for any blind hockey team to operate they need to have about 20 pucks on hand, and that's about a thousand dollars. As a result, a lot of players practice with really messed up pucks. While there have been several efforts over the past 10 years by universities and private citizens to create an alternative, ruggedized puck, none of them have yet succeeded.
3. The third rule change is that the attacking team, while still having to obey the offside rule, must also complete a clean pass before they are allowed to score. This rule is designed to prevent the players with the most sight from dominating by going end to end with the puck. It also gives the goalie and defending team a fair chance to find the puck in case the players on one team have a lot more vision than those on the other team. Those ball bearings in the hollow metal disc make a racket as the puck is slapped from one blade

> to another and as it bumps and bangs over the ice. Once the referee decides a pass by the attacking team is clean—that it went from one attacking player to another without deflection or interference by the defenders—the ref blows a special shrill "pass whistle" to indicate the attacking team is now allowed to try to score. The process seems cumbersome, but you can still have a lot of bang-bang goals. Usually the attacking team tries to complete the required pass early so they can play normal offensive hockey, cycling around the zone, or even running a play, but a tap-in goal also counts as a pass. This issue of a "clean pass in the attacking zone" has become the most frequently debated issue in blind hockey, with endless arguments about whether a pass met the criteria. It has also created an interesting style of defense, as the defending team can guard passing lanes while allowing the skater with the puck to circle, circle, circle, and eventually tire themselves out. All the defenders have to do to disrupt the attack is to tip a pass, because then it doesn't count as clean. We call that "dirtying up the pass," and most of us can hear when it's clean or not.

These rules remained flexible for a long time. For instance, when I started, the completed pass rule was after the red center line, but we changed it in one tourney to the attacking blue line, much closer to the goalie. It aligned with the offside rule and was easier for the referees to call and led to fewer controversies.

Although the sport of blind hockey is only about a decade old, by bringing more people into contact with it we hope to eventually elevate blind hockey to a Paralympic competition. That is probably still a decade away, because a critical mass of countries must be able to field competitive teams to qualify a sport for the Paralympics. This means that all of us current players, in addition to enjoying the game for ourselves, also feel we are long-term entrepreneurs, ambassadors to a next generation who think that someday, perhaps, someone else's kids might be playing blind hockey in the Paralympics. There's probably an eight-year-old in Minnesota dominating his Squirt-level league who will, for some reason or another, get eye disease. I don't wish that on anyone. But if it happens, then someday I'd like to think that he or she might compete in the Paralympics. Will they know the Saturday mornings we spent in D.C. trying to build a first American team? Or the efforts then to expand to other markets like Denver or Minnesota or Hartford?

Thinking ahead to those future days, I imagine an eight-year-old now skating happily in Minnesota or Boston who has an underlying genetic condition and will, someday, be blind like me. My first hope is that he'll be cured without having to go through what I've gone through. My second hope—if that's not possible—is that the hard work I put in helping build the sport of blind hockey will allow him an opportunity to be a Paralympic athlete, an opportunity I'll never have.

I think once blind hockey makes it to that level, it'll be the most watched Paralympic sport. It's way closer to the speed of regular hockey; twice the speed of, say, sled hockey. It looks and feels a lot more like what most people expect hockey to be, compared to other adaptive versions of the sport. There are things like quad football, or quad rugby, which are definitely cool. But the speed, combined with the realization that everyone playing on the ice has less than 10 percent of their vision, will make blind hockey the most entertaining para sport in those future Games.

Chapter 4

OPENNESS

Refs have a particular sensitivity to being called blind. Yet had they ever been called blind by an actual blind skater?

IN 2010, THE COMPANY WHERE I WORKED, Booz Allen Hamilton, went public. In quick succession thereafter, it underwent a massive management layoff, reducing payroll costs to make its stock more attractive. For the first time since I was 15 years old, I was without a job.

From 1992, when I first started bagging groceries at my local Harris Teeter, all the way through my time at the Air Force Academy, where as a cadet I drew a small paycheck, up until this momentous layoff in 2012—even while I was going blind, even while I was in graduate school, even during the recession of 2008, even while switching industries or deciding whether to go into academia or not—I had never been unemployed. To this day, the two-week period I spent after Booz Allen has been the longest I've gone without working. From one job to the next I always ended up with people approaching me, telling me they had opportunities, asking me to look into this or that position. People saw my talent. I am grateful for the ease with which I have moved up the corporate ladder. But at that moment, in 2012, after 20 years of steady and increasingly hefty paychecks, for the first time in my adult life I didn't know what to do with myself. The layoff caught me by surprise.

Not only that, but I had also established myself as the breadwinner in my marriage with Brita, working hard to put her through her MBA program, just as I had promised her parents I would. We'd also recently signed a mortgage on our first house, and Brita had a hankering to spend some time studying abroad in Turkey.

The pressure built to a fever pitch inside me.

I'd never yet in my young career applied for a job. I'd never thrown a million résumés out to the wind, just to see what might stick. Recruiters or people I knew from my network always found me. Now, I discovered the desperate feeling of having to search for a position. I needed to support Brita, and I didn't have the time or mental space to think about what I really wanted. Therefore, when a friend approached me and asked me to help with a NASA project, I didn't overthink it. I jumped at it. While it sounds a little bizarre, plunging into a role like this without too much forethought, it did have a nexus with my background in supply chain logistics. Our nascent team was going to develop and pitch a new process to NASA for how to launch cargo into space from the old Soviet space center in Kazakhstan, thereby resupplying the International Space Station.

At the time I remember thinking to myself: *I've never launched anything into space before, but how different can it be from other forms of supply chain analytics I've worked on?*

This all happened a year or more before I started playing hockey, but the feeling of beginning this job and beginning to ice skate were similar. In the same way that, emotionally, I needed the outlet of hockey to keep growing and challenging myself personally, I needed the outlet of this new work opportunity to keep growing and challenging myself in my career. Yet the new job, in comparison with learning to skate, came with the added pressure of needing to eat, keep a roof over my and Brita's heads, and support her while she was in school.

As good as this opportunity appeared to be, it ended up morphing into something I didn't expect at all.

First, while I gave my heart and soul to this team for four months to complete our proposal, we didn't win the bid. I never actually worked a day launching stuff from Kazakhstan, much to my disappointment.

But what ended up happening during the writing of this proposal proved just as critical to the future of my career.

We spent four months together, a small team laboring day and night over the details of launching things from the middle of nowhere in Kazakhstan. In the world of government contracting, only about 10 to 20 percent of people are any good at writing proposals. Of those, most hate it. It's a notoriously labor intensive and nitpicky art form. Perhaps less than half the people who are any good at proposal writing are ever willing, more than once or twice, to dip their toes into that sort of work. I was lured in by the uniqueness of Kazakhstan and the glamor of being associated with NASA and the International Space Station. Yet, once I put my nose to the grindstone, I didn't let the difficulty of proposal-writing get in my way, even with my blindness as a factor.

I started the project by helping gather the team, identifying a number of small companies in the D.C. area who could contribute to the logistics involved. One of these, Akira Technologies, had just been launched by a man named Eli Liang. As we built the proposal, Eli and I started to naturally gravitate toward each other. We locked ourselves into an office in Rosslyn, on D.C.'s southern beltway, for the majority of the four-month proposal-writing window. During this crunch, in order to meet some of NASA's deadlines and jump through various gates in the proposal process, we often ended up sleeping in the office—Eli kicking his shoes off and leaning back on a big leather chair in the conference room, me on an inflatable mattress I purchased and used in my temp office down the hall. We worked late and we started early, even before coffee at 5:00 or 6:00 AM. Eventually, we finished this project together, but we cut it so close to the deadline that we had to send one of our team members on an airplane hand-carrying the proposal to Johnson Space Center in Houston to turn it in on time.

I had been hoping to get a bonus for winning the contract, so when we found out we were not selected for the work, I felt pretty deflated.

However, a couple weeks later, Eli—with whom I had fought and bled to produce the Kazakhstan proposal—called me up to tell me he admired the way I worked, especially since I had to put in three times more effort than anyone else due to my blindness. He'd seen me up close and personal, sometimes for 24-hour stretches, often unshowered, unshaven, and at a time when the stress of my work and my lack of work-life balance started giving me ocular migraines that made one eye or the other go completely blind for long stretches of time.

In contrast to Brita, who only knew I was sleeping at the office, unaware of the depths to which I was sacrificing to support her, Eli saw something in me.

He suggested I help him with a new proposal to revamp the firewalls of the Defense Logistics Agency's (DLA) computer systems. While I had only limited experience in the excruciating work of government contract writing, I still felt the sting of losing what had been billed as a "stable" job at one of the "Bigs"—Booz Allen. Working for a smaller, more vigorous company appealed to me. I signed on with Akira, Eli's company, for this one project, negotiating a low-dollar contract that at least kept me working.

We won the DLA firewall contract and, frankly, when we did it surprised everyone—to the extent that Akira would rather not divert the cash to pay me what we'd agreed while at the same time gearing up to execute the work. In a win-win move, I told Srini and Eli to keep the cash; took a stake in the company; and joined the team on a permanent basis, becoming Akira's chief operating officer, a new and expansive role for me.

Being open to taking on the shitty work, doing the drudgery of proposal writing for a government contract, had a lot of parallels with learning to play hockey. I had the sensation, in both, of groping in the dark, of exposing myself to something not just new but largely unknown. I experienced a willingness, even an expectation, of failing, while developing the resiliency to try and try again. While we had certainly hoped our four months working on the NASA bid would have resulted in a win, neither Eli nor I had really counted on the DLA contract to come through. The same for those first hockey lessons: I wasn't really counting on them leading to anything in particular. Who would have thought that I could actually learn not just to skate but to play the sport's fully sighted regulation rules when I had only started to participate in the sport as a grown and legally blind adult?

Most adult blind hockey players come to the game via the following steps: they learn the game growing up fully sighted and they play until they're diagnosed with an eye disease or, through some other accident or quirk of fate, lose their vision. Their hope for continuing to play hockey disappears at this moment, until they hear about blind hockey.

I don't know of anyone who was born fully blind and then learned hockey. I'm one of the few who went blind and only after that decided to learn to play the game. There's this guy I know named Daniel Belding who was a pretty good regulation hockey player up until bantam, the youth hockey league term for those aged 15 or 16, and then was diagnosed with retinitis pigmentosa, one of the most common eye diseases that hockey players have. Some of the others are Stargardt disease, which is what I have; Leber hereditary optic neuropathy (LHON); aniridia; and albinism. Some estimates have Stargardt disease occurrence as rare as 1 in 100,000 people, so when I walk down a street, I know there's almost no chance I'll run into someone else with Stargardt. But when I walk into a hockey locker room, I know there's a good chance I'll meet two or three others.

Three of my favorite hockey players, Nate and Aiden McCown and Anthony Ciulla, are albinos. All amazing athletes and all great human beings. Albinos are very desirable hockey players because they're born with generally overall fuzzy vision right around the limit of legal blindness. As a result, a lot of them learn to play as children in regulation hockey, then qualify for blind hockey later. Albinism results in relatively stable vision for a person's whole life, so once they learn the sport, they don't thereafter have to struggle with ongoing degenerative vision. Most people who have a degenerative-type eye disease follow a similar pattern. Everything is hunky dory for them as a kid, as it was for me. They then find out really bad news in their teenage years or early twenties, including whether they're going to be able to continue to participate in sport. Where I differed from this model was that I never played hockey as a kid. I went blind and learned to play as an adult.

Most adults who learn hockey later in life, even those who are fully sighted, don't get a chance to play competitively either. A really good outcome for an adult learner of the regulation game is to eventually play in something like a lower C-level beer league. Making a competitive team like Team USA is a huge outlier for an adult learner, something I don't believe has ever been achieved in the regulation game.

One of my advantages in this was that I chose, almost by accident, to start in the very beginning of my hockey career to play fully sighted regulation hockey, rather than restricting myself to blind hockey. I really had no choice in the matter. Back in 2013 when I started, there just weren't blind hockey teams. I had to put my nose to the grindstone to learn the game, just as I had done in learning to write government contracts. And just as I overcame those challenges, through failure and gradual incremental victories, I began to skate regulation hockey before I had the opportunity to help lead the creation of competitive blind hockey programs in D.C. and around North America.

Here's what it's like playing fully sighted, regulation hockey as a blind person.

Just like I mentioned when learning to skate, much of what I've experienced comes with a feeling of frustration. As an example, I got tagged with a penalty for unsportsmanlike conduct for jamming my stick at a goalie's glove. The goalie didn't have the puck covered, which is the moment when the play should stop. Instead, the puck clearly sat beside him, on the goal line. While it is always a matter of fine-tuned interpretation for a ref to blow the whistle or not blow the whistle in such a situation, I still knew the puck was still loose, as did all my teammates. My mistake was to yell out, "What the hell, man! *I'm* blind and can tell that the puck wasn't covered."

It's a trope to call the refs blind, of course.

People wear Three Blind Mice shirts to games. They bring blind canes for the refs. They wear dark sunglasses like Stevie Wonder. So refs have a particular sensitivity to being called blind.

Yet had they ever been called blind by an actual blind skater?

I was proud of my witticism, yet also angry. The ref probably didn't even know I was visually impaired, and that was one of the nuances I began to pick up: the fact that they couldn't actually tell. To them, I just seemed like another rampaging idiot beginner, barely under control on the ice.

I'd get penalties a lot for charging, get called for offside a lot. I'd run into people or jump over the wrong boards. When I began to understand that refs couldn't tell I was blind—that they just thought I was reckless, a bit of a loose cannon on the ice—I made myself learn to approach them quietly before games, during our warm-up laps. I'd find a moment to tell them something like, "Hey guys, I'm trying to be as safe as I can out here, but I am mostly legally blind. Please tell me if I'm doing something dangerous or trying to go onto the wrong bench. Otherwise, just call me for all the normal rules. I appreciate being treated just like any other player, as much as possible."

Being a little more vocal about this took me out of my comfort zone and took a little time to learn and incorporate as a process in my warm-ups for the games, but it ended up helping me develop a relationship with and appreciation for the refs.

I also tended, as I got a couple years into my actual journey playing competitive hockey, to join teams and leagues slightly below my actual skill level. I mean, I was and am blind, so that evened the scales a bit. But I do remember one game, as an example, where I picked up the puck in my own defensive zone, wheeled around, skated through the entire defense of the other team, beat the last defenseman, and shot up and across the goalie's body. The other team's bench rose in unison, yelling at me for being a "ringer"—a player too skilled for that particular league. They continued to chirp at me the remainder of the game, not knowing about my visual challenges. Then, when they were standing around afterward, they had to watch me get in a MetroAccess handicap cab to go home from the rink with my blind cane in my hand. I couldn't hear what they were saying, muttering amongst themselves, but I felt both a sense of frustration and satisfaction at this turning of the tables.

I admitted to myself that I had gotten, probably, too good for that particular league, at least when—or if—I ever got the puck on my stick, just as that moment of skating the length of the ice demonstrated. But my opponents didn't know how difficult it could be for me to find the bloody puck in the first place, or that catching a pass with a regulation puck remained almost impossible for me. That'll happen once or twice a game, almost on accident. And the breakaways, the long rush with the puck across the whole length of the ice sheet, occur no more than once or twice a game as well, and result in a goal even less frequently. So there's a dichotomy of being better, yet not being able to find the puck or play the game the same way sighted players can. Is it fair? Maybe not. But I continued to play in these leagues as my skills improved.

Another thing that turned out to be more difficult for me than for sighted players: distinguishing some visual cues while on the ice. For example, when a goalie wears a white jersey, I have no way to know where to shoot. I probably score 90 percent of my goals against goalies wearing colored jerseys, because I can't ever really see the net behind the goalie. I therefore don't aim for the net. I simply shoot for where the goalie isn't. If the goalie wears white, with white boards and a white net behind, I've got no idea what I'm looking at. It's all just a cloud of whiteness. Same with white jerseys for my teammates or the opposing team. I lose all chance of telling people apart from the ice or the background glare. Often teams have two colors of jersey, a darker one for playing away and a lighter color, sometimes white, for their home rink. If that is the case, I ask the other team if they'd consider not wearing their light-colored option. This requires a bit of debate, and of course a lot of explanation, but usually teams are happy to do that—as long as their players brought both sets of jerseys with them to our game!

I also have to spend a lot of time teaching new sighted teammates how to play with me. There's a learning process involved. For instance, when I'm standing across the ice from them, waiting for a long pass, it doesn't work for them to send it directly to me. I can't pick up the black dot of the puck in time to catch it. However, if they bounce it off the boards first, I can more often locate it on the ricochet, hearing it hit the boards and then making a good guess where it is going as I track the sound of it sliding over the ice, a very faint hissing compared with the ball bearings in a blind-hockey puck.

The other half of this experience of competitive hockey, for me, is that of playing in blind hockey games as one of the few skaters who also regularly plays sighted hockey.

First of all, I say "blind hockey games" rather than "blind hockey league" because there is no real blind league.

As of 2024, the Canadians are trying to start such a league, but they haven't launched it yet. Instead of league play, organized blind hockey is more like a confederation. There are local teams, but they don't typically play each other one-on-one. If they did, the best programs would be able to field a whole team while other cities would only muster one or two people. The guy I think is the best blind player right now lives in Grand Rapids, Michigan, and he's the only blind player out there. If we played league play he'd have to commute to both away and home games, probably to Pittsburgh. That's too far for any one person. Instead of having geographically arranged teams, the way we play competitively is to practice together at "home rinks"—usually ones affiliated with and sponsored by NHL teams, but then we all drive or fly to a host city for tournaments. When we arrive, we take stock of who had made it to that particular weekend's festivities, then scramble players onto teams, making each team as evenly matched as possible. This might result in a total of 15 or 20 competitive games in a calendar year. The remainder of our hockey experience consists of local practices and scrimmages.

For both American and Canadian blind hockey players, as for players around the world, getting to play for your respective national blind hockey team is a life-defining moment, even if the games themselves tend to lean heavily toward the Canadians being the better team. Winning the Canadian national championship is also special in its own way. When I was playing, this was represented by the Courage Cup.

I ended up winning two Courage Cups, the second one in 2022, five years after the first one in 2017, with my time on Team USA sandwiched between. The two times I won, while playing with the Canadians, form a kind of bookend for the meat of this life phase of playing competitive hockey. (I'll cover both of these experiences in greater detail in later chapters.)

Another fun tidbit about blind hockey: the names of the teams are often quite creative.

In Calgary, the team chose the name Seeing Ice Dogs.

The Hartford blind team, modeled after the professional NHL Hartford Whalers (now the Carolina Hurricanes), is called the Hartford Braillers.

Our team was the Washington Wheelers (with a logo I designed myself). Wheelers is a tongue-in-cheek reference to the fact blind people can't drive. The logo features a blind man on a motorcycle with his seeing-eye dog in the sidecar of the motorcycle. Working on designing that logo was quite an adventure, because I had the idea for it, but then had to hire an overseas graphic designer while trying to found the D.C. team. Some NHL teams, like Hartford, will allow the blind team to use or riff on their name; some won't. The Minnesota Wild and Chicago Blackhawks allow their disabled teams, both blind and sled, to use their name and logo in their branding. The Washington Capitals won't. The Pittsburgh Penguins won't (the Pittsburgh team is called the Rhinos). The Avalanche won't allow the logo to be used, so the blind team is called the Colorado Visionaries. None of the teams in Canada will let their blind affiliates use their name or logo. Therefore, Canada has the Toronto Ice Owls and Montreal Hiboux. Both mascots are owls. But they are, really at heart, the Maple Leafs and Canadiens of blind hockey. The team in Vancouver is called the Eclipse.

The Carolina Hurricanes–affiliated blind hockey team takes the cake, though, in terms of best blind hockey name. They are the Carolina Blind Canes.

I'm probably a C-level hockey player when competing in local regulation beer league play against sighted players. But anyone who can play competitive sighted hockey at all will be one of the best couple dozen blind hockey players in the world right now. That has proven to be the case with me. The experience of learning the regulation game, not even to the extent of dominance but of competence, puts me pretty high among all the blind hockey players in North America right out of the gate.

For sighted players, a tier of hockey akin to minor league baseball exists. Players can go to this right out of high school or even earlier. It's called Junior A, major junior, or sometimes AAA, depending on which region in North America. The best blind hockey player, Jason Yuha, had been playing Junior A in Alberta when he started to lose his vision. So far, there are no professional NHL players who became legally blind and then joined us playing blind hockey—but gosh, wouldn't that be the dream for our Team USA, to find a dominant player who competed at the Division I level of college hockey at a place like North Dakota or Minnesota, or who played some Junior A? I'd never wish blindness on someone, but if that should happen, and if the person still wanted to skate, we'd love to enlist such a ringer on our team!

Chapter 5

TRUST

*The differentiator of truly successful people, to me,
is the ability to focus even in the midst of distractions.*

BUILDING TRUST QUICKLY is an important skill I've learned, equally applicable in a locker room and a boardroom.

In blind hockey, quick conversations built around shared experiences are a key to the whole process. Except for at the national team level, all blind hockey tournaments use the scrambled roster format I mentioned earlier. That means I might land in Toronto on a Thursday night, take my blind cane (which I'm using because I'm traveling alone through an airport I don't know well), my hockey bag, and my sticks—held in the same hand as my blind cane—half a mile across Toronto Pearson Airport, jump into an Uber to get to my hotel next to the old Maple Leaf Gardens, and only find out at the registration table that I'm playing with guys, and perhaps a few gals, from places as disparate as Halifax, Calgary, Chicago, New York, and a bunch of other towns and cities. This group will have not much longer than three or four hours to build trust before we turn in for the night, only to play a game together the next morning against a team that is, fortunately, also made up of scrambled players who are largely unknown to one another. To win, you've got to jell quickly.

Even prior to participating on these teams, blind hockey provided me with another such opportunity to build trust quickly, and it ended up being one that helped shape the sport of blind hockey for a lot of people.

At a bar in Alexandria, Virginia, in the winter of 2015, I came across a hard-to-miss blind man. Doug Goist is 6'5", has the wingspan of a pterodactyl, and is known to enjoy a cocktail from time to time. The first moment I met Doug, he stood against the rail at an Irish bar trying to get himself a beer. It's a situation familiar to every visually impaired person, or at least every such person who goes to Irish bars. First, in the back of our minds we're asking ourselves, *Is there even a bartender here?* We can't see if that's the case or not, so it's a legitimate question. As both a blind person and a lover of a good bar, it's a question I find myself often asking, given the fact that my limited vision often won't allow me to know I'm about to be served until a bartender says, "Hello."

Once we confirm that fact, one way or the other, we next must ponder a few additional things, all in rapid succession:

Is this dude looking at me?

Should I randomly yell in order to get attention?

Do I raise my hand like a kindergartner who needs a pee break?

All of this in the aim of simply getting a brewski.

Normally, if I'm in a bar, I'm too focused on not knocking people's drinks out of their hands or running them over to notice other patrons. But Doug was impossible to miss. I'm 5'10", and his blind cane stands taller than me. At the time, in late 2015, I was two years into my first-ever stint as chief operating officer, working for that start-up tech company, Akira Technologies, which had just won the Defense Logistics Agency firewall project. I was also in the very earliest stages of ideation for another start-up, thinking about putting together an organizing event, with the Washington Capitals, that would eventually lead to the formation of a blind hockey team I named the Washington Wheelers. I was on the lookout for talent for both fledgling projects—and, as anyone who's ever run a start-up knows, quickly building trust is essential to recruiting. So, I saw Doug; muttered to myself, "That might be my goalie;" and made my approach, quickly deciding that I'd smooth things over by bribing him with beer.

It worked like magic. Doug is now the starting goalie for the U.S. National Blind Hockey Team.

But he didn't start that way. He started as a stranger in a bar. If he were the one telling this story you'd probably get some version of "Craig tricked me," followed by his equally impressive and interesting road toward becoming a competitive goaltender.

As I approached him, barside, I noted that he had gotten no closer to procuring his drink of choice. I said, "Hey man, need help getting a beer?"

I then explained to him that I could barely see myself, but that I'd managed to learn the bartender's name, so I didn't have to visually locate the dude. I learn names quickly and do so with intention. It's a trick I often use with waiters, bartenders, and colleagues in all walks of life, so that I don't accidentally try to flag down the wrong person. Plus, people just appreciate that you know their names. This bartender's name was Dan. I hollered his name, he came over, and we got Doug a pint. I carried it, along with one of my own, as Doug took my elbow and I led him to a nearby table where we could talk.

At the time, I was single. So was Doug. I'd been a former athlete before I lost my vision. So had he. Doug worked in tech. I did too. About midway through the conversation, I brought up my idea—just a crazy thought at the time—of starting a blind hockey team in D.C. Doug laughed. He thought I was joking. I wasn't sure I was serious at the time, either.

By the end of the conversation, Doug and I had agreed to meet at an ice-skating rink the following week. I earned enough of his trust that he let me, a legally blind man, escort him onto the rink at the Georgetown Waterfront in D.C. so that we could try skating together. I'd only been skating for about two years at this point. Certainly I was no pro. But I was able to confidently explain to Doug, in the type of detail only a blind person can formulate, the mechanics of a skating stride.

After that session, Doug agreed to join "a few other friends" and me for an event in February 2016 with the Washington Capitals, where Doug, who is completely blind, let a stranger put goalie pads on him and maneuver him in front of a hockey net while other strangers shot the heavy, ball-bearing-filled blind-hockey pucks right at him.

Doug thought about leaving the ice right then and there.

But then a six-year-old blind boy tried to slap one of those special pucks at the net. Doug moved his pad to let the puck slide across the goal line. The young blind boy scored his first-ever goal and raised his hands in celebration. At that moment, Doug didn't feel the cold, wet sensation of the melted ice that had soaked the jeans he was still wearing under his pads, and he didn't feel the pain of the impact from several errant shots that had hit him. He felt his heart leap at the fact that he'd just helped a blind boy experience one of the best moments of his life.

Doug didn't need to trust me anymore from that point on. He had a new feeling in his heart that could take him the rest of the way, buoying him.

And so, the man who would eventually start in net for the U.S. National Blind Hockey Team—a man who had never played one second of hockey in his life before that day—fell in love with the idea of being a goalie by intentionally letting in a goal that he'd remember for the rest of his life.

A few years earlier, the same tendency to quickly build trust served me well in the development of a tricky but glorious business relationship, demonstrating the skill's transferability between sport and business.

The episode happened back in 2008 at a place called Buddha Bar in Dubai. Buddha Bar was the sort of joint that felt like an earthly incarnation of Star Wars' infamous Mos Eisley Cantina, albeit with humans rather than aliens. Music pumped, smoke swirled, a feeling of danger and also of great opportunity wafted through the seedy, post-colonial air. Walking in the door, all eyes would turn on the newcomer. The music would seem to stutter, stop for a moment. Gulping, the visitor would either be forced to quit, to extract himself, fleeing on entry, or would need to plow forward, despite knowing everyone was watching him. Then after a moment, the person would blend. The miasma would engulf him. Things would settle. And the newcomer would become just another part of the backdrop.

Buddha Bar was packed most nights, at least after 10:00 PM, with expat businessmen of every type—Western, Asian, Arab, Greek, Russian—all hanging out in small groups, talking about deals they'd done, deals they dreamt about doing, places they'd been, laws they'd flaunted, risks they'd run. Brazen squads of upscale prostitutes from a matching variety of nations stared down the laughing, cajoling men, watching them like tigers watch fresh meat, looking for any sign or invitation. Eye contact of any sort meant that one or two of these ladies would peel away from their companions and approach. Drugs were likely being consumed in the shadier corners, despite Dubai's harshly prohibitive laws. And, of course, alcohol flowed freely, with glasses clinking, bartenders shaking silver tumblers, corks popping—again, despite Dubai's strict laws against buying or drinking alcohol in most places. This, however, was a Western place. A tolerated place. Booze was legal enough, though the whole artifact of its presence felt a lot like a speakeasy, somewhat seedy but frequented by all the decision-makers anyway. Incongruously, though, it wasn't an old saloon-like building. Those don't exist in Dubai. Instead, Buddha Bar tried to create this atmosphere even though it occupied part of the ground floor of one of Dubai's many new hotel skyscrapers. Outside its large windows light from the greasy warm water of the Arabian sea danced amid the fingers of docks where dozens of high-end yachts tethered.

I loved going to Buddha Bar. And I loved a particular drink there called the Flaming Lamborghini. I was in a wild phase at this time, an impulsive phase—attracted to anything shiny, fast-moving, or unique. Both the bar and its signature drink, which the bartender would turn into a pillar of dancing blue flame by igniting its fumes, ranked high on the scale of glittery fascination for me.

I'd come to the United Arab Emirates to help build a huge sustainable urban development near Abu Dhabi called Masdar City. My vision had gotten bad enough that I no longer drove, so I'd hired someone to take me everywhere I needed to go. Before arriving in the UAE, I learned how software could help measure and optimize sustainable living by talking to building management systems, point-of-sale systems, and energy grids to allow humans to live more sustainably. My employer at the time, Lockheed, sent me to the Massachusetts Institute of Technology (MIT) for a certificate in this type of work, but other than that, I had no particular experience in the field. I was a virgin at sustainable systems architecture, yet my role would be to design and implement one of the biggest ones in the world. This was still early in my career. By applying the same scrappy attitude I'd developed around sports—always being the try-hard kid who raised his hand for the dirtiest and most difficult assignments—I realized I could get ahead of peers who might be more talented or credentialed. I'd take these hard assignments, like living abroad, traveling as a blind person not only to a place without much support for the blind but also on many work trips to the UK, Belgium, the Netherlands, and Silicon Valley, and I'd do so almost as a way to prove to myself that I wasn't going to let my lack of eyesight slow me down.

During this time, my status as an ice hockey fan continued to develop (though I'd not yet conceived of the idea of stepping on the ice myself). Air Force's hockey team was in the midst of a renaissance, making the NCAA tournament for the second time. I would have to use a VPN to get American sports channels and then listen to the games streamed over the radio late at night, right into the wee hours of the morning, hooting and hollering from the tiny balcony on the 12th floor of the apartment tower I lived in. No one cared. Most of the apartments had suddenly gone empty, with the market crash of 2008 that came about from the Lehman Brothers investment firm and the associated real estate collapse. That year, Air Force beat Michigan in the tournament, a huge milestone and one that was doubly important for me, since Air Force was my alma mater and also my mom still worked for the University of

Michigan. The scene couldn't have been better for me, despite the strange circumstances of my location as a fan, chugging beers and wearing Blue and Silver Air Force paint on my face, all alone on that 12th floor balcony of my apartment.

In comparison to this lonely fandom, I craved (and found) social shenanigans of the sort Buddha Bar provided. The drink Buddha Bar had invented, this Flaming Lamborghini, involved a martini glass with a strainer placed horizontally over it and a tall bottle of Galliano balanced on the strainer. The bartender mixed fruit juice and rum in the martini glass then poured absinthe into a brandy snifter, lighting the absinthe on fire and pouring it down the sides of the bottle of Galliano. The lucky customer would use a plastic straw to drink from the martini glass while fire poured into it. I loved everything about this experience because it was something I could see. It caught my attention. It pierced through the haze of my failing eyesight to make an impression on me.

One such night, I was whooping it up, making a scene of myself, buying these drinks made of cascading fire for everyone around me, when I noticed a nearby group of men also buying Flaming Lamborghinis and doing so in perhaps even more of a flamboyant manner. Members of that group kept looking in my direction. Eventually, one of them approached me.

"Are you a celebrity?" the man asked.

I laughed aloud. I was many things by then—a former Air Force officer, a wannabe athlete, a disabled vet, a man uprooted from his country, pursuing a new career and willing to go to the ends of the world to achieve some sense of success and self-worth. But I wasn't a celebrity in any sense of the word.

Then, like the flaming drink I still held in my hand, the impression of another man seared itself on my mind's eye.

It takes a lot to break through visually for me, but I caught an unforgettable flash as this man came into the limited area of vision at the far-left corner of my field of view: an exotic-looking man, not exactly white but not brown either, and with an amazing shock of curly hair extending in all directions from under the edges of a natty old Ferrari baseball cap. He wore round professorial spectacles and had a dimpled chin along with dark eyes that flashed with intelligence. He was speaking fluent Arabic to those around him, but as he neared me he switched into English—the Queen's English—thick with the smooth sounds of Oxford, yet with just the faintest Middle Eastern accent under it. (Later, I learned that this man had attained fluency in 11 languages.)

"Well," the man said, "you may not be a celebrity, but you sure look like you're having the most fun of any of us here."

"I'm here all the time. I live upstairs," I replied, pointing to the ceiling where, as everyone in Dubai understood, the glass and steel floors extended upwards another 40 or 50 levels.

Hearing my accent, he said, "American?"

"Yup," I said. "I was an Air Force officer."

"Awesome," he said. "I was in the U.S. Army for a spell myself."

This surprised me but built instant trust. We started down that well-worn path of comparing war stories: where we'd been, who we'd worked for and in what conditions, stupid stuff we'd seen and done, trials and tribulations, boondoggles and shenanigans. His list ended up being by far more impressive than mine, since I'd been forced out after five short years, and he'd attained enough prominence to work in the Clinton White House.

After a bit of this, he asked, "You a tech guy?"

"Yeah. I'm here working on Masdar City for Lockheed Martin."

"Me too," he said. "I mean, I'm in tech. But not with Lockheed."

This turned out to be the understatement of the year. He was in tech in the same way that Mario Lemieux or Patrick Roy were in hockey. One of the good things about being mostly blind is that I'm not often awestruck in the same way sighted people are. I have no idea who I'm talking to, unless I've had a proper introduction. This guy at the bar with me, who had just then turned to the bartender to order us up another round of Flaming Lamborghinis, hadn't been introduced in any sort of formal way. Maybe I had an inkling, already, because of the gentle initial approach from one of his crew. But the signs that someone has made a bunch of money, that he runs one of the world's most famous AI programs (back then, in 2008, in its very early days), aren't as apparent to me as they might be to others. I couldn't see the way others looked at him, fawning over him. I just treated him like a normal person—and I thought that became part of the charm, my charm, really, the naïveté and bonhomie of a new American friend around whom this man could drop his guard and have an honest conversation.

He finished ordering the drinks and turned back to me. I could see him size me up, his head nodding a bit, north and south, as he looked at me from the toes upward, then settling back at my face again. I was in good shape at this time in my life, working out daily, almost as muscled as one of his bodyguards.

"Do you know the source of inspiration behind the name Flaming Lamborghini?" he asked.

"No. I just love 'em. The fire. The flash!"

"Well," he said, "in Islamic banking you can't charge interest. So all the newly rich Westerners here, especially the ones who come over starting up this or that business on some quick venture capital bucks they gathered together, when they buy a fancy car in order to 'make sure they create the right impressions in Dubai business circles,' they have to hand over checks signed for each month of their installments. It's a little weird but a workaround so that everyone feels secure about the purchase. Only thing is that..." here, the bushy-haired man waved his hand around the room, which I took to mean—back then in 2008—the way that Lehman Brothers bank had failed and the markets had begun their headlong crash that signaled the start of the Great Recession "...like now, when things have gone to hell, these get-rich-quick investment streams suddenly have a problem on their hands. They've beaten their Lambos and Ferraris up pretty good, and they know they can't make the payments anymore, even if the dealership holds those pre-signed checks. So they take them for one last spin, blowing all the red lights on Sheik Zayed Road, racing each other, racking up thousands of dollars of tickets. Then, literally, they park out in the desert, get out a gas can, and set their cars on fire so the car dealerships can't cash the remaining checks. They board one-way flights out of Dubai before the authorities catch up."

"Jesus," I said.

"Or, better yet, one might say *Yah Allah*," the man joked, softly shaking me by the shoulder. "It's not just Westerners. It's the Lebanese, the Syrians, the Russians, anyone and everyone who overleveraged themselves and tried to live the fast and loose lifestyle."

We went on to talk a little more about our jobs, our pursuits, our interests in life. And I learned his name. I won't use it here, but let's call him Nelson Howell. He founded a well-known technology think tank and a groundbreaking lab that is a collaboration between two of the world's top scientific universities. He was also a professor of computational neurology and functional neurosurgery, inventor of a potential cure for Parkinson's Disease via human-computer interfaces, and a soon-to-be billionaire entrepreneur (once he, unlike many others, recovered from that 2008 crash). He told me none of this at Buddha Bar. Instead, we jumped into the sort of immediate friendship that I'd learned to make through my early years of competitive sports and my abbreviated military career—the sort of connection that proceeds swiftly and then calibrates itself later, if necessary. Nelson knew that game, that style, having begun his career in the military too. So we were on known footing, at least in this particular mode of trust-building.

We closed down Buddha Bar. He invited me to his penthouse at the top of the Horizon Tower in Dubai Marina for an afterbar. It sounded like fun.

His condo nearly recreated the Buddha Bar, but in classier style: white couches and panoramic windows filled with people, the interesting oddities collected from his travels and lifetime experiences. Whereas Buddha Bar's aesthetic tended toward the Mos Eisley Cantina, his penthouse reflected something more akin to Lando Calrissian's Cloud City. Nelson proudly displayed a high-end Stradivarius violin, which he had taught himself to play. Music, like the 11 languages he knew, came easily to him, basically another and more soulful language. Yet, though we each took a drink with us from his sprawling bar, we didn't hang out with the rest of his after-party crowd. I found it much more interesting to talk about big ideas in a social setting than just get drunk and gossip.

We spent the rest of the night in his kitchen, sketching plans for the backbone architecture of my Masdar City's sustainability data system. I had no idea that I somehow co-opted a world-famous computer scientist into my effort, but Nelson seemed to be enjoying himself, so I wasn't going to stop him!

I hadn't been working in "real" tech for long at that time, and I found out that night at Nelson's that, just like in sports, the readiness to prove myself at a moment's notice, to strap on the metaphorical skates and leap over the boards into the fray, served me well. I'd spent months and months learning how software architectures work, what a software development life cycle involves, and how to think about technology finance. In doing all this, I applied the principle of practicing hard while no one was watching. It enabled me to leap at the opportunity that now presented itself, holding my own as Nelson and I sketched out ideas on the back of several sheets of paper on a kitchen counter. Sometimes, you know when your big games will come: a gold medal opportunity, a tryout, a scheduled board meeting. But sometimes you don't know—and the ability to jump headfirst into unscripted moments has gotten me just as far as showing up for scheduled events. I didn't shrink from that moment with Nelson, but I'd also put in the time beforehand, working on my shot, my skating, all the preliminaries. I didn't know then how impactful this relationship would become, but I was ready for the chance of it.

I was still single at the time, and there were plenty of beautiful non-pay-for-play women at the afterparty, but I ignored them all, as did Nelson, while we sequestered ourselves in his kitchen. The party swirled around us as we both tacitly agreed we'd rather spend our time plotting technical specifications than chatting up a drunk Australian flight attendant. I find that in sports, tech, and business, the most successful people don't do it for the fame, the money, or to get laid. We do it because we genuinely prefer work we're passionate about, and if fame, chicks, money, or Nobel prizes come as a result—so be it. The differentiator of truly successful people, to me, is the ability to focus even amid distractions and even as a little taste of success fills the air. At that moment I'd already made it to the Emirates, which was a mark of success in and of itself, at least in my mind. I'd already landed a high-paying job and I was working on fairly high-end, potentially world-changing tech. I was fit, smart, and had largely overcome the possibility that my vision would hold me back. In fact, it even started to dawn on me as a bonus, my inability to see the temptation of the flight attendants in Nelson's living room. My lack of eyesight improved my ability to focus. It helped me keep my mind present in a moment that ended up setting up much of my career thereafter.

Returning to the theme of the Lehman Brothers crash, Nelson described himself, in a moment of sincere vulnerability, as one of the many members of the new "former multi-millionaires club" He also told me he'd just returned to Dubai after a whirlwind two weeks abroad, reassuring his own investors, propping up the financing for his Emirates-based projects.

Maybe Nelson had already sized me up, by this point, as different from the 50 or so other Western businessmen partying that night in his condo, not just some cliché expat looking to party my way through the Dubai experience. We'd built trust quickly. We shared a military background, a technologically invigorating present, and the ability to tune out distractions.

This is perhaps why, a few days later, at about nine o'clock in the evening, he called me. It was definitely unexpected. I didn't think I'd ever hear from him again, though I'd given him my number and business card as a matter of form.

But there he was, talking rapidly on the other end of the phone line.

He explained the situation in a few brushstrokes.

One of his several start-up companies had purchased a Ferrari and a Mercedes G-Wagon to serve as company transportation. Most companies in the UAE must be 51 percent owned by Emirati citizens. For this reason Nelson, like all other businessmen in Dubai, had involved a local family as co-owners. The Emirati "investor" listed on the documents as co-owner was 20 years old. Part of the Flaming Lamborghini generation, he had grown up during the era when Emiratis received an oil-funded stipend. During Nelson's few weeks abroad, shoring up the trust of his investors, he'd left the company in the hands of this young man who proceeded to take both the Ferrari and the G-Wagon, rack up thousands of dirhams in camera-recorded speeding tickets, all in Nelson's name, and get the G-Wagon flagged for impoundment if ever it were pulled over. So the young man and his father, who was the real head of that family's business enterprises, apparently deciding that Nelson would likely not come back to Dubai at all after his trip to shore-up the nervous investors, claimed the G-Wagon as collateral against the business and removed it from the business' parking lot to their family compound's gated backyard.

I suppose, in addition to the quick trust we'd built, Nelson might have also valued the fact that, since I had been working out like a fiend and had gotten pretty jacked, with a buzz cut, a mid-American accent, and a military background, I might be intimidating to an out-of-shape 20-year-old Emirati. He asked me to come to a business meeting with him, at the Address Hotel in Dubai, where he was going to get back his car, set his bank accounts straight, and see if he could still do business with this Emirati family. His only ask of me was to just sit there, be quiet, and stare at the kid. I had figured out by then how to look people in the eye, even though I couldn't see their eyes. I just listened for the location of their voice and directed my gaze three inches higher.

We arrived at the hotel about a half-hour late, doing so on purpose because Nelson wanted to keep the kid waiting. We walked in and I shook the young man's hand a little too hard and for a little too long, saying hello but making the point of why Nelson had asked me to be present. The meeting lasted two hours and was conducted almost entirely in Arabic. I had no idea what Nelson was saying—probably lecturing the kid on the business, the vehicles, ethics in general, trying to decide what to do next. Nelson made it a point to turn toward me every 20 minutes or so and say a sentence in English such as "you don't take another man's property" or "trust is more important than money."

The meeting stalemated. The kid seemed too afraid of his father to say yes to giving back the car and paying the tickets, or maybe he was just too entitled to condescend to Nelson's pragmatic demands. I could neither understand Arabic nor read facial expressions, so I had only the faintest idea of where the argument stood when Nelson got up, apparently agreeing to go to the family's gated estate, riding together in the back of this kid's car, to continue the negotiations directly with the dad.

After driving for a while into the heart of one of the better, plushier neighborhoods of Dubai, servants opened a gate in the back of one of the compounds—and, luckily for us, these servants left the gate partially open (more on this in a moment). We climbed out of the kid's car and sat down on plastic lawn chairs in the middle of their well-watered, almost fake-looking green lawn.

The kid stayed involved, but the conversation now only really involved Nelson and the father, a man who may as well have been a cartoon: vastly overweight, wearing a wife beater tank, sitting with his feet up on an Igloo cooler as he drank cheap beer and chain-smoked. A stack of beer bottles littered the lawn at his feet. I couldn't count them, but I heard him kick one over as we sat down. I couldn't see the compound itself, nor determine whether the feeling of being watched meant that there were actually other people around, perhaps observing us from a balcony, perhaps watching from the compound's windows. I couldn't see any of that, but the effect came through clearly for me. We were, quite literally, on this family's turf. This slovenly man's rules applied. Nothing else mattered. I couldn't tell if the father was armed. But I knew that a well-connected family in the Emirates could get away with murder if they claimed it was justified and I guessed that the attempted reclamation of a company car might qualify. The thought that I might die struck me as, suddenly, a non-zero probability.

Luckily, this time, most of the conversation shifted to English.

"Nelson, Nelson, my friend," the father said with unctuous tones. "You left the country without assuring us that our company's assets were secure. The G-Wagon is now ours. We will shut down the company, deport your employees back to India, and part ways. We've moved the remaining assets out of company bank accounts as an additional precaution. Surely you understand."

Nelson did not get angry. He simply said, “No, I don’t agree to that. You don’t take another man’s property. I told you I was leaving to secure our position with our investors, and I told you that I would return. You had no right to begin withdrawing assets and seizing cars.”

The conversation continued like this for about another 90 minutes, during which time I counted another seven beers consumed by the kid’s father. Voices began to rise. The argument escalated and I sat there trying not to look scared, wondering what I’d gotten myself into.

Finally, Nelson stood up, turned to me, and said, “Craig, let’s go.”

I assumed we were going to call a cab, or start walking.

The father told his servants to shut the gate, and told us that we weren’t going anywhere.

Then something happened I hadn’t counted on. Nelson pulled the spare key fob for the G-Wagon from the pocket of his coat.

I didn’t even know the G-Wagon was nearby, but Nelson grabbed me by the arm, encouraging me to stand. I heard the click of doors opening on the vehicle. Assessing it to be about 30 yards away, I started running toward the click. Nelson got into the driver’s side. I dove through the open passenger door and the vehicle took off before I could close it behind me. The G-Wagon was about 100 yards from the gate, and luckily the servants decided they didn’t want to die as the vehicle reached ramming speed. They stopped closing the manual, barn-style, double-door gate, throwing themselves bodily to the ground on either side. We cleared the gate, screeched out onto the road, and turned right before realizing we had no idea where we were. GPS hadn’t yet been integrated into smartphones back at this time, so we drove around for about 45 minutes, trying to find our way back to Sheikh Zayed Road and to the Marina and Nelson's Horizon Tower condo.

Nelson called another of his in-country business associates, a Russian named Sasha, and he joined us at the condo. It was now about 3:30 AM, a Friday, and though UAE businesses normally do not operate on Fridays, I worked for Lockheed, an American company, and was expected to be in the office that morning as a result.

Nelson, Sasha, and I assessed that the G-Wagon would be reported stolen even though it was registered in the name of the business Nelson and this Emirati family had opened. Further, we guessed that in any dispute with authorities over whether a crime had been committed, the Emirati family would win. So, we decided on the following Flaming Lamborghini–inspired plan:

A. We'd drive the G-Wagon to a parking garage in Dubai Marina, a location commonly used to ship cars out of the country. There we'd park it and throw a cover over it.
B. We'd walk to the nearby Barclay's Bank branch, one of the few banks commonly open on Fridays, and withdraw whatever funds remained in Nelson's company accounts.
C. We'd file an emergency application with the Indian embassy to prevent the deportation of the company's employees by granting them temporary work visas.
D. I'd let my boss at Lockheed know I'd be a little late for work.

We got to Dubai Marina around 5:00 AM and found a cover for the G-Wagon. Nelson did his thing with the bank when they opened at 7:00 AM and we called my driver to come pick us up and take us back to Sasha's place, in case anyone came to Nelson's penthouse looking for him.

I had a couple shots of vodka with Sasha to calm my nerves, drank two cups of coffee to keep myself awake, then went downstairs, where my driver waited to take me to work. Luckily, I was able to make it a short day, and I finally got to sleep a little after 3:00 PM.

The follow-up from that story is the impactful part. I earned Nelson's trust that night. We began to have conversations about professional ethics, technology, right and wrong, finance—lots of stuff I'd always wanted to learn since I had grown up without a dad. I now consider Nelson a big brother. He appointed me as a Fellow with his think tank, which uses AI to bust illicit networks around the world. Nelson also officiated my first wedding a few years later. Though the marriage to Brita didn't work out, I have kept the fellowship because I bring some business know-how, technological knowledge, and work ethic to the team. I've given my time to the think tank for almost 15 years now, and being involved with that nonprofit has made a positive difference for me mentally when, from time to time, my regular work hasn't felt all that fulfilling. I became a Fellow not necessarily because I was a super talented AI scientist, but because I built a relationship with Nelson based on trust through the wild rehoming of his Mercedes G-Wagon.

Teams that win build trust quickly.

With my blindness I am constantly confronted by the need to do so more quickly than most people—both on the ice and off it. To succeed in a sighted business world or with new blind teammates, I need to jell very quickly with diverse people. I think one of the reasons I've won more than I've lost in blind hockey tournaments is that I've learned to build trust quickly. I've learned to take chances, even seemingly irrational ones, and be willing to be let down more often than not. I'm not afraid to be let down by someone I trust. Losing my dad at an early age, I felt very let down. In life I've had a lot of letdowns—going blind, the sudden unexpected end of my military career, the collapse of my first marriage. By being less afraid of the possibility that somebody will let me down, I believe it is easier to start from a position of trust. That has been true for me in sport pretty much all along. The best team players are trusting. You'll send a pass to a player whether he is going to bury the pass in the back of the net or not. You'll share the puck. Even when you make a pass perfectly—flat, on the money, right there on the other player's stick blade—and he flubs it, you learn to trust that guy again the next time. You trust him as a matter of principle. And by trusting in that way, you help build trust across the team as a whole.

I feel that same instant application of trust mirrors what I did with Nelson the night I agreed to go renegotiate his G-Wagon with him.

Chapter 6

TEACHING

Striving for and achieving proficiency at something by learning to teach it has been a secret to my success, not only in hockey but also in business and life.

I MOVED SWIFTLY FROM LEARNING TO SKATE, which I undertook simply to give myself something to focus on outside of my work and my failing marriage to Brita, through the process of understanding the basics of the actual game of hockey, and from there right into league play. One of the perks of that Rockville learn-to-play-hockey course was that those who survive it—I say that somewhat euphemistically; no one actually died during the course, though a few people drifted away and chose not to complete it—and finish the course are immediately formed into a new team at the lowest, entry-level tier of the Rockville rink's beer league.

When our cohort reached this stage in the developmental course, the three coaches who had been instructing us for the past two months came into our locker room. They congratulated us and unveiled our team name—the Rockville Rebels—and jerseys. We'd earlier been given the choice whether to continue with the program and join the team or to opt out. They sweetened the deal by including the fees for our first four games as part of the learn-to-play course. They knew that pretty much anyone committed enough to slip and slide and fall down all over the ice as an adult beginner hockey player would want to continue through at least one season of play. This four-game allowance provided an easy transition into their league and kept prospective clients of the beer league, and the rink's programming, hooked, rather than letting them slip away to competing leagues, some of which might have been closer to the learners' homes.

Now, invariably, one or two of the players in a course like ours will have played at least some hockey growing up. These folks will have taken the course more as a refresher, a way back into the sport, rather than joining up as true rookies.

That was the case for our Rockville Rebels team. One of the guys, Jim Mangani, had grown up skating in Boston as a kid but, now in his forties, found himself in the midst of a midlife crisis. This led him back to hockey. As a result, when our instructors in that same congratulatory meeting in the locker room asked us to nominate team captains, Jim won in near unanimous fashion. Everyone pointed at him. He was the best player on our team. We all slapped our sticks on the ground—choosing him by acclamation.

Jim journeyed out the 45 minutes from D.C. to Rockville for the course, just like me, so he often provided me a ride. We got to know each other pretty well during those trips. About halfway through the season, he told me he was gay. Coming out like that, in the midst of a hockey season, took courage because, like in many sports, you shower together in open locker rooms with your teammates, a bunch of mostly grown men. We were strangers to each other and that probably presented even more of a challenge for Jim than for the rest of us. It's not like going through an experience with schoolmates where you know them through all kinds of other walk-of-life stuff, seeing each other daily in third period science class as well as on the rink. I empathized with his experience, having often felt the need to explain why I was different because of my visual abilities. Jim gradually told the other players on our team too. And I realized that this Rockville team likely accepted me more, with my visual issues, because they also accepted the idea of being led by a gay captain. Hockey has come a long way in accepting disabled, LGBTQ+, and other nontraditional players since 2013—but at the time, I still considered this to be particularly brave on Jim's part, and we bonded over it.

I assumed I wouldn't be good enough to make a difference for the team on the ice. I thought I'd be just as likely to run into someone as to make a pass or score a goal. So I resolved to try to make a difference in the locker room. My schtick throughout the eight-week course, my angle to start doing this, involved being the guy who always brought beer. This challenged me because I had to drag a heavy wheeled cooler a mile or more from my house to Union Station, carrying my sticks and slinging my hockey gear in another heavy load over my back, and I had to do this for every practice where I hadn't been able to arrange a more direct ride. Beer formed a part of my plan to help support the team. But I had a number of other approaches as well.

For one, I hit the books hard.

I treated every hour on the ice as a chance to learn.

I researched the nuances of the game and found resources for drawing up hockey drills to teach myself the fundamentals of skating, passing, stick handling, shooting, and positional play, and then I studied these drills until I understood what they were trying to achieve and how I might apply them. Book learning is good, but it needs to be put into application to have any effect. In order to put my learning into practice, I began to invite other members of the team to independent on-ice sessions, taking advantage of slots on the rink's calendar called "open ice" when anyone could show up, usually at really odd hours of the day, and pay a small fee just to skate, practice, or form up into ad hoc teams for a bit of scrimmaging.

During these sessions I would often seize a small corner of the rink and with two or three of my new teammates, whoever could join, plus any other random skaters at the open ice session who showed an interest in what I was doing, I'd run through some of the drills I'd unearthed. Now, to teach those drills, I printed up sheets of paper beforehand with the instructions spelled out in big letters even though, on the ice, I couldn't read the words. I prepared in advance though, memorizing not only the drills but also the order in which I'd put the sheets, doing all of this during the 90-minute train ride up from D.C. to Rockville when I could have my laptop open and zoom into the PDFs to make the finer points of the text large enough to read.

While Jim was the obvious choice for captain—he was after all the best skater, the best with the puck, and, as the season progressed, the team's highest scorer—we still needed to pick two assistant captains. In his first act as captain, Jim stood in the locker room and asked us who they should be.

My friend Andy Ashcroft knew I'd been a flight commander in the Air Force and knew I could lead. I hadn't talked about that with anyone on the team, as I spent most of my time pretty steadfastly focused on trying to learn the game and its skills. I also consciously chose to put the military part of my life, and with it the focus on my disability, into the background. I don't like to talk too much about my time in the Air Force because I find it can quickly become an excuse for a lot of disabled veterans and disabled people in general, an excuse that prevents them from experiencing and achieving new and good things. I don't want to be known for what

I used to do, or for what my limitations are, but for what I can do now and what I have the potential to do in the future.

Although I didn't emphasize my military background, in this case the background mattered, at least to Andy. Compared to the other beginner hockey players on the team, I had some formal leadership training and experience. More importantly to me, I thought that my present leadership mattered to the team. Organizing and showing up for those additional open-ice skating sessions, being the try-hard guy at every practice, and taking pride every session to be the first guy in the locker room and the last guy out, having that attitude and determination in the present moment, meant more to me than my military background.

Plus I brought the team beer.

It all added up and when Andy nominated me, the room agreed pretty quickly.

I was honored to wear the 'A' for my first hockey team, the Rockville Rebels.

The third guy chosen was a dude named Nate Cook, not a bad choice either. He was a welder who had played some roller hockey. He understood the game's concepts more than others.

Even having been chosen as one of the captains, I still believed at this time that there were many things in hockey I wouldn't be good at because I couldn't see the puck. However, I also knew I wouldn't always have to have the puck on my stick to play good positional hockey and make at least a little difference. I resolved to become what I like to call the "glue guy."

Anyone who is a fan of hockey, or really most sports, can probably imagine what this "glue guy" does and is—a member of the team who tends to be a third-line grinder but provides great morale and brings the team together. Just watching the sport on TV, it might be hard to pick this guy out, but now, as I tuned in for Avalanche or Capitals games, I started keeping tabs on how these players operate and what terms knowledgeable folks use to describe their play.

For one, a coach or a sports announcer might say that a skater has a strong "north-south game." What this indicates is that a player makes a commitment to go straight up the ice without being overly fancy when his team has the puck. To me, at this time not being a talented enough skater to move laterally on the ice very well, and therefore not being able to try any fancy stuff, I decided to work hard to make my legs strong enough that I could skate fast in a straight line. Then I figured out I could watch other players head toward where they thought the puck was, follow their line, and beat them to it. This brought me close to understanding and playing a style of hockey similar to the north-south game I'd been hearing about.

A second term for the try-hard glue-guy that I began to hear was "leaving it all on the ice." To me this meant that in hockey a clear division existed between skill play and effort play. Skill play is a beautiful thing, maybe a dangle through a couple of guys to set up or score a goal, fancy stickwork to weave around someone, deception or speed, perhaps strength or quickness in a shot. An effort play might be something more like the chaotic time when your team turns the puck over to the other team and you've got to haul your ass back to your defensive zone in case your defensemen get beat. Especially in beginner hockey, when so many players are afraid to make any plays at all, I learned quickly to focus more on the effort and awareness aspects of the game than on silky smooth skill plays.

A third such term, related to "leaving it all on the ice," is when an announcer or coach calls someone a "committed backchecker." This means skating as hard in defense as in offense and doing so all the time. There's a temptation in hockey, like in most sports, to work hard in the glory moments: to be the guy who dunks the basketball, closes the game out as a pitcher, or catches a touchdown. Yet most contests in team sports are won in the trenches. It's a beefy lineman gaining an extra inch of leverage to create a hole for his running back. It's the guy on defense who forces a driving point guard to pass the ball away rather than reach the rim. It's the fielder diving for a line drive or hustling to beat out an infield single. In hockey it's often backchecking—returning to the defensive zone as quickly and with as much hustle and desire as when on offense.

This first team of mine, the Rockville Rebels, got the shit kicked out of us for our initial season, even in the lowest, most beginner level of Rockville's beer leagues. But we kept practicing. We kept organizing and, whenever possible, three or four or six or ten of us would show up for the same open ice practice sessions I'd started during the eight-week course. In our second season we lost our first five games, then suddenly won a game by a score of 9–1, a blowout in hockey terms. In our open ice session we'd been practicing one simple type of pass that could facilitate a break-out play, rehearsing over and over again how to get the puck out of our own defensive zone and transition into attacking the other team. In our first victory this pass resulted in numerous breakaways and several of those nine goals, revving us up and getting our momentum going. We kept it up, even going on a 14-game winning streak, winning the league, and getting invited to Toronto to play in a Hockey North America tournament—basically an unmitigated success for a beginner team like ours.

The interest I sparked in myself by studying the game, by finding and printing out and teaching other players on the team the drills I found, blossomed after this.

I started thinking through the possibility of launching a blind hockey team in D.C. at this time, and I arranged a meeting with the management of the NHL Washington Capitals team. I knew they already supported other forms of disabled hockey, such as sled hockey, and I hoped they would donate to my blind hockey idea. Yet, when we sat down together, they immediately told me that funds were limited and had already been committed to the sled team. They couldn't support my effort monetarily. But what they could offer me was ice time, at the horrible hour of 6:00 AM. At least this would be in a more convenient location for me than Rockville, Maryland—a rink in D.C. itself, which was then known as the MCI Center and later became Capital One Arena.

The only problem I had to overcome in accepting their offer of free ice time? I needed a USA Hockey–certified coach to show up at that god-awful hour for the team's insurance to cover us during our time on the rink. I couldn't find a coach willing to do this, despite many attempts. So the idea came to me that I could just get my coaching credentials. I therefore embarked on a familiar path—becoming a coach and teacher of a subject even as I learned to master it myself.

This process, of striving for and achieving proficiency at something by learning to teach it, has been a secret to my success not only in hockey but also in business and life. It's a technique I use because, more than other people, the need to internalize information and to be able to communicate it clearly rises to prominence in helping me overcome my blindness. I can't simply visualize a concept or a piece of information the way a fully sighted person can. I tend to hear things first and see them second. Whereas a lot of other people backstop their ideas by accessing reference material or using the internet to find and confirm information in real time, I challenge myself to internalize how a concept works and I do this exactly because the act of reading and researching requires much more effort for me than for a sighted person.

For instance, the rules for teaching quantum physics—which I've now learned in support of my present role with SandboxAQ, an AI and quantum computing company—and those for teaching hockey do not organize themselves all that much differently in my brain. Both are very complex concepts. To master those skills myself, to master the performance of them, the doing of them, I've found that moving forward to teach them helps me improve with incredible speed. And it's not just a nice-to-have skill for me, an abstract issue. It's a survival skill.

I took lots of physics classes in high school and as part of my undergraduate studies at the Air Force Academy, but never any specifically on quantum physics. So I enrolled in MIT's courses on quantum computing and quantum algorithms when I took the SandboxAQ job, becoming the first blind person to pass MIT's program. This was even tougher than it might sound, because a lot of the work writing algorithms and solving problems occurs via study and production of three-dimensional diagrams, not something a visually impaired person usually handles with ease. Yet, after I started giving presentations and lectures on quantum physics, including a recent one at American University, the abstract became more concrete. The diagram I might have wrestled with conceptually transformed into a teaching prop, a framework I filled in for others and thereby solidified in my own mind.

I've deeply integrated my learning in other fields this same way, too. When people ask I can give directions turn-by-turn to anywhere in D.C. from the Washington Monument—which reinforces the memorization of spatial patterns, necessary at small scale so I don't run into things in my own house and also at large scale so I can find my way around a city. I like giving directions to places around D.C. to challenge my own knowledge of where I am, where others are, and how to get from place to place. I've done the same internationally by creating solid mental maps to help me navigate places I've worked, like Brussels; Abu Dhabi; Dubai; Windsor, England; and Austin, Texas. Similarly, I mastered supply chain management after my stint in the Air Force, working for Maersk, where I designed and taught a game whose principles were invented at MIT through studies of a thing called the bullwhip effect in system dynamics.

Among many other examples from business and life, I also took profound joy in learning to cook and in teaching my siblings to cook too, well before I lost my vision. This joy in teaching, and the experience of teaching as a means to learn, thus has its wellspring back in those earliest days, more in my role as caregiver and father figure for my siblings. It simply blossomed and became reinforced in my methods as I learned to overcome my blindness.

In all these areas, the fact of my visual impairment could have been a detriment. I made it into a source of advantage to myself, my employers, and my family.

One last instance of teaching, as mentioned a few chapters ago—I also had to teach fully sighted players on the regulation-league teams I joined. I didn't teach them the game of hockey so much as I taught them how to play hockey with a blind person. There weren't any instructions for this. Playing with a blind person was a novelty for them. But figuring out what would help me most, and then teaching it to my teammates, absolutely became a crucial thing for me.

In addition to the example from earlier—telling these fully sighted players to bounce the puck off the boards for breakout passes to me, allowing me to hear it rather than just try to see the blur of it—I developed a few other tips and tricks to help my sighted teammates play better with me.

Perhaps the most important of these involved various aspects of verbal communication. Loud verbal communication.

I asked my new teammates to focus on calling me by name when they wanted to switch on the fly, which is a unique hockey tidbit wherein play does not have to stop for players to swap out from the bench and join the action. Calling by position, which is fairly normal—saying "Hey left wing, switch out"—didn't work for me. I had enough to remember with all the other things going on in my mind, tracking the puck, the constantly shifting positions of the players (so I wouldn't run into anyone), the location of the boards (so I wouldn't crash into them either), my proximity to the pesky blue line, etc. So they learned to say "Fitzy, Fitzy!" when they wanted me to switch. It took a lot of reminding and several too-many-men-on-the-ice penalties, but once my teammates figured it out, the technique ended up becoming a bonus for everyone and an enhancement for our coordinated movement about the rink. We all became more aware and more verbal in our bench-to-ice communication. We got to know each other better. And as a result, compared to other teams composed of grown men calling each other by their position rather than by their names, we ended up bonding more closely and playing better together.

Likewise, if I went back for a puck, especially when playing on a more advanced team, certain plays could be run.

Sometimes teams would do this by a glance, or just by watching how and where other players set up on the rink. Of course, I couldn't do this. But because of my need to verbalize everything, my linemates learned to yell cues to each other, the names of plays like "Wheel!" or "Reverse!"

Even if I wasn't capable of making the play, I got people to yell the names of these maneuvers at me once I'd mastered the concepts of them in my first year or two of competitive play. In fact, I learned after a while that if I happened to have the puck on a breakout and was able to work up some speed, I could predict in my mind's eye where the opponent would attack us. That "Wheel" call meant that somewhere halfway between my own net and the boards, if I came up the ice with speed, I'd have a 50-50 shot of getting a first move on someone, switching the puck forehand to backhand. And I could soon do that without even thinking about it, allowing me to beat the first attacker myself. Then I would have six feet of freedom in front of me. The opponent's left wing, stationed along the boards to try and control the puck's flow, would be on my right, against the wall, so I only had to visually queue up the locations of two more opposing players. One of these would probably be somewhere on the blue line in front of me and another would trail me off my left shoulder. I would, in this schema, end up in the clear for a break-out, a key moment, and—with a startling level of accuracy—my mental picture and the visual picture of the world that I couldn't fully decipher tended to coincide. I could listen for my teammates calling for a pass ahead and I could, therefore, play a meaningful part in attacking, which is a great feeling, being not only a solo player, trying to be in the right position, but elevating my game to the point where I became part of a cog in a larger, coordinated, synchronized machine.

The same applies when I play defense. When the puck comes up the boards and I'm trying to hold the offensive zone, it's important to prevent the puck from crossing the blue line and making our whole team cycle out of the zone before going on the attack again. I've taught my defensive partner in this situation to yell at me, provide warning of the puck's approach, and to do so by calling my name. Then I know to start trying to find the puck.

Catching a pass is still a lost cause for me, though, unless it's a blind puck with rattling ball bearings that I can hear. I can start to expect to see a regulation puck when it is beside me within about 10 feet. My peripheral vision extends about that far, down and to the side out of the corners of my field of vision. However, if a pass comes directly at me, it's gone.

It doesn't exist. It emerges out of the cloud of my vision as nothing but a sound, slipping past, far too fast to allow me to react. The sound of a regulation puck striking the boards and the angled approach of the puck through my peripheral vision is my best bet, especially if the passer has called my name to alert me in advance.

All this learning and teaching of the game prepared me for my next big endeavor. As mentioned, I jumped in with both feet—as organizer, player, and also coach—of a totally new thing for the D.C. area: a blind hockey team.

Chapter 7

TAKING A RISK

*Although I sensed more and wanted more from hockey,
both as an outlet from work and as an escape
from the feelings of solitude after my divorce,
I didn't know what those next steps could be.*

THREE MASSIVE THINGS HAPPENED concurrently leading up to and during 2015.

First, Brita and I divorced. We'd been separated for a good chunk of 2014 but finally took that step in October. Because of this I began 2015 with emotions from the divorce still raw. I felt a keen need to work through them while remaining resilient.

The second major thing had to do with my job. Whereas 2014 felt like a chance to dip my toes into the world of entrepreneurship with Akira, early in 2015 my two partners—Srini and Eli—decided to pursue a spectacular growth trajectory. This allowed me to throw myself into the company, which was good because I had a lot of energy and wasn't quite certain where to direct it. I wasn't quite ready to go back into the dating scene yet, and all that energy needed to go somewhere! I chalked up 2014 as primarily a year focused on losing a marriage while trying not to lose the nest egg of my growing business success at the same time, throwing my lot in with Akira to build a framework that would allow us to create a lasting company. As a result, 2015 would become the year Akira took off, even though I knew I'd have to grind hard to do my part in making that happen.

The third major facet of the year involved hockey, of course. I assessed 2014 as the year I moved beyond being a novice player. That growth was awesome but painful. I took formative steps to become a "real player"—both on the rink and in the corporate world.

We won our league in Rockville during that same winter of 2014–15—those glorious 14 games in a row I mentioned before. Then the summer of 2015 came around and my Rockville team traveled to Toronto for the Hockey North America Championships. All this happened alongside the massive growth sprint at Akira. I took my job so seriously that I put a cot in my office and, though technically still living in my previous marital home, along with two dogs, I signed a lease with a tenant who agreed to do dog care so that I could live day-to-day in a room at a friend's house, closer to the office. This way I didn't lose time commuting across town every day. In the six months between April and October 2015, Akira wrote 51 responses to government requests for proposals and won 17 of them, while the Rockville Rebels won the league in April and I played in Toronto in the summer. It was a crazy time but also exactly what I needed to prove to myself I could survive the divorce.

Somewhere in the middle of this, while working those 16- to 18-hour days, maybe making it back to my house on Capitol Hill for a night or two on the weekends, I ended up spending a particularly restless night. I was supposed to be working on one of those government proposals. But I'd just returned from the Hockey North America championships and had taken part in my usual Tuesday night on-ice skills clinic, hosted at the Caps' rink for intermediate players who were continuing to hone their abilities. I had spread all my gear out and covered the surfaces of the balcony in the bedroom of my friend's house, airing out, drying.

I looked at that equipment and asked myself: *What are you still trying to get better for? What are you still trying to do with regard to hockey?*

I knew I'd reached the point where my skating sufficed. I could step on the ice with just about any crowd, any group below Junior A or true college-level players. I had learned how to shoot. I could hit the stick blade of one of my teammates from 30 feet away with a pass, at least if the person had tapped their stick on the ice to draw my attention to where they were. But I still couldn't catch a pass.

My vision continued to create problems in regulation hockey. Staying onside remained a continual bugaboo. Figuring out specifically where to shoot when I approached the goalie puzzled me, as I often couldn't see the goalie or the net against the background whiteness of the boards and the ice. So, putting my Akira work aside, at least for a few indulgent moments, I began to google whether any assistance for blind hockey players existed, whether anyone else had been going through these same challenges. I hoped to find a community, or maybe just one or two people like me I could talk to, someone who had maybe done something similar. I felt stuck, like I had reached a plateau. Although I sensed more and wanted more from hockey, both as an outlet from work and as an escape from the feelings of solitude after my divorce, I didn't know what those next steps could be.

I went down a deep rabbit hole that night trying to find another legally blind hockey player. Unspoken, but there in the back of my thoughts, the real question I was trying to answer was probably this: *Have I done everything I can do in hockey and should I turn my focus to work and work alone? Is that what life has in store for me?*

Eventually, somewhere in the bowels of the Googleverse, I found an article about two people in a small town in upstate New York: Kevin Shanley and Christine Vanturini, both blind, both very interested in hockey. They had just started an organization called Courage USA to try to get blind hockey going in the United States. Their problem was that they lived in the middle of nowhere, a place called Newburgh, which is almost exactly an hour and a half due north of New York City and an hour and a half south of Albany, with the wilderness of the Catskills filling all the intervening space. The math, for how to field enough blind people with the skills and desire to start a hockey team, just didn't work out for them. Starting a blind hockey program would be tough in a major metropolitan area, let alone in a hamlet of Newburgh's size, with a population of less than 30,000. (The total U.S. population is 333 million, of which 1 million are blind. That means Newburgh probably had a total of 90 or so blind people of all ages and interests. How many of them would really be interested or able to play on a hockey team?)

Regardless of their odds in this effort, Kevin and Christine were the best leads I found that night. I emailed both and then went back to my proposal writing, feeling like I'd at least done something to assuage the feeling of being alone, of plateauing in hockey, of wanting some sort of wider connection and understanding about what I was going through. The work with Akira gripped me again, so I didn't think much more about these emails or this lone night of frantic research. I pushed hard through the rest of the summer of 2015, working myself to the bone and keeping up the routine with hockey, even though it had started to feel hollow.

To this, I added another pursuit—trying, once again, to date. As the litany of my shattered work-life balance already shows, I didn't really have time for much of that, but I gave it a try. I allowed myself to go out on either Friday or Saturday nights, but not both. Of course, those nights involved booze and they centered on trying to meet a girl. Then I'd go back to work the next week, maybe sneaking in hockey on a Saturday night from time to time. This was the routine as the summer of 2015 came and went.

Just after my 39th birthday, in October 2015, an email ping finally returned from the ether, Kevin Shanley responding to my message from earlier in the summer. It came with a short-notice call-to-action.

"Hey Craig," he wrote, "I just saw your email. Thanks so much for reaching out. We're actually having the 2015 U.S. Blind Hockey Summit up here in Newburgh on Halloween weekend. Would you like to come? There'll even be ice time at the rink here."

I'd formed some plans for Halloween already, but they seemed, strangely enough, to align. I'd scheduled a weekend off from work, off from hockey, intending to go to Manhattan, where I'd stay with a single friend of mine and hit the party scene Halloween Eve. Kevin Shanley's blind hockey summit started that next Saturday morning.

At this point in my life and in my hockey career, I didn't know what blind hockey was. I'd never heard of it. I went searching for it on the internet but, compared to now, there wasn't much video or explanatory material out there to explain the sport.

But it was exactly the sort of connection I'd gone looking for. I thought to myself, *Okay, let's give this a whirl.*

I took the Megabus from D.C. to Manhattan with a full set of hockey gear. I suppose that could have been my costume, if it didn't smell so authentically of the locker room. Instead, I bought a costume on arrival in New York: a pink tutu, a pig mask, and a pair of suspenders.

I went through with my original plan to have all the fun I could in Manhattan on that Friday night. Then I shoveled myself onto a train from Manhattan to Newburgh, bleary-eyed and barely functioning the following Saturday morning. These were the early days of Uber too. My plan at the time I left Manhattan involved a train ride from NYC to Newburgh followed by the normal Uber from the train station to the ice rink. Living in D.C., which Uber had already colonized by then, I'd started to take the service for granted. But in a 30,000-person town like Newburgh, more people probably still knew Uber as a term from Nietzsche rather than as a ride-sharing app. It just wasn't an option yet in small-town America.

I ended up calling the rink. I asked if they knew anything about a blind hockey summit and I heard a really deep folksy Canadian voice come onto the line after a few seconds. The man asked me if I was Craig. He said, "I've heard a lot about [*aboot*] you. I'll be right there to the train station to pick you up."

I was stunned. Small towns might not have Uber, but they had a personal investment and a willingness to help that I didn't normally find in bigger cities.

The voice on the line, it turned out, belonged to a man named Matt Morrow. Matt has been the executive director of Canadian Blind Hockey for a decade now. Back in 2015, though, it was early days for blind hockey, even in Canada, and Matt went himself to every individual event across the

U.S. and Canada trying to grow the game. He's fully sighted but was involved in jobs during school that involved athletes with a disability, then worked with the Canadian Blind Sports Association for a while before venturing into leadership of blind hockey in his home country.

Ten minutes after my call to the rink, Matt arrived to pick me up. I believe I was visibly hungover, perhaps even still drunk. I'm certain he could smell the fun I had had the night before. During the few minutes of this drive, though, he managed to elicit a few key facts from me, namely that:

(a) I had less than 10 percent of my eyesight left.
(b) I had not quite two years of experience playing hockey.
(c) I had only heard of blind hockey two weeks previously.

We got on the ice in Newburgh. I took a few warm-up laps, and on my trip around the goal I ended up turning hard behind the net and I lost an edge, slamming headfirst into the net itself—taking out the goalie who was warming up in the net, another player who was trying to skate behind the net, and generally creating something like a 10-car pileup in a NASCAR race. Struggling back to my feet, I shook it off and tried my best to continue the warm-up skate. I have to imagine that Matt Morrow, with whom I'd spent the trip to the rink blathering on about how well I knew the game of hockey, probably thought I didn't belong on the ice. It was pretty embarrassing.

I ended up sweating out the fumes from my revelries of the night before during a few initial drills. Then we scrimmaged.

I found out pretty quickly that the Canadian guys who had come down, from both the Toronto and Montreal programs, numbered about a dozen, so we had enough to play a two-way scrimmage. More than that, I also realized I could keep up with them. It took me about half the first scrimmage to get a feel for the blind puck, that huge metal cylinder I'd never before encountered. And it also took me a while to understand how the Canadians cleverly employed the rules of blind hockey to outwit those who didn't know what they were doing. By the second half I discovered that stickhandling the heavy blind puck wasn't a good idea. Instead, the cup-and-carry method, which is also a good method in regulation hockey—simple and straightforward—really helped me pick up speed while also keeping the puck quieter. This made it harder for other players to find the puck and steal it from me. I scored my first goal during the opening moments of our third scrimmage period. Matt, who was refereeing, fished the puck from the net, handed it to me, and told me to keep it as a memento.

This puck was mangled. At the time I had no idea how expensive they were or how tough they were to obtain, so the details of this award, its real honor, passed through my still-addled brain like a ship in the night.

We played a while longer, then got off the ice, had a few meetings, and suited up again for a second scrimmage that afternoon. I put in a couple more goals as I began to integrate and understand the rules of the blind game better. That evening we all reconvened for a banquet. I had the beat-up dented puck in my bag and felt good about the possibility of being able to play blind hockey. I was looking at the sport purely from the perspective of my personal involvement, my personal participation. I didn't know much about the state of the sport across the country. At the end of that dinner, Kevin Shanley pulled me aside and said, "Listen, Craig; Christine and I are trying to grow this game and we're talking to USA Hockey already, but there's just the two of us and we're in a small town in New York. What would you think about starting a program in D.C.?"

That was how the idea came about for me to start a team. I said yes on the spot, but I didn't know the first thing about starting a beer league hockey team, let alone a 501(c)(3) charity and an entirely new hockey program, in a new version of a sport, which would require resources, organizing people, educating, teaching, coaching, mentoring, fundraising, and all kinds of other time-intensive activities.

I came away from the event motivated, though.

When I reached the comfort of my little rented room close to my workplace in D.C., I immediately cold-called the head of Public Relations for the Washington Capitals, a man named Peter Robinson. It took me a few tries to get through to him. Professional organizations are pretty protective of the phone numbers and contact details for their senior management team. I was cagey with the lower-level people about why I wanted to talk to Peter Robinson, not wanting to be brushed aside by someone with a little power but no decision-making ability. When at last I got Peter on the phone, I opened up more, telling him that I had been playing at the Caps' rink for a long while in one of their leagues, that I'm blind, and that I hoped he might help me host a "Try Blind Hockey" event under the auspices of the pro team.

Peter thought about this proposition and said, "Well, we have this thing in February called Hockey Is For Everyone month. And we're already doing an event for special hockey, which is for kids with special needs. It's a joint thing with a charity called Dreams for Kids D.C. We've got a big block of time for them, and it sounds like they won't need the ice for the whole period. Would you want to maybe use the ice right after them?"

I said, "I think so. But I don't know. I've never organized a hockey event before."

As a result, I began my new endeavor, that of blind hockey organizer, with about 90 days' notice between that call in early November and the offer of ice-time booked for the following February. I needed to kickstart a new organization, recruit players or even just curious blind people to try it, and get the gear we needed—because USA Hockey enforces safety rules stipulating that you have to wear a helmet if you're on the ice, and that you need skates and sticks for everyone. I developed a long list of things I needed to get done. But even before Peter and I hung up that first call, he asked, "What organization should I put the ice-time reservation under?"

I said, "I don't know. Can I get back to you tomorrow?"

That night, all alone, I brainstormed and came up with the name Washington Wheelers, because blind people can't drive. I found it funny and ironic, and I also hired an online graphic designer to put on paper a logo I dreamed up for the team: a seeing-eye dog sitting in the sidecar of a motorcycle.

Immediately after this call with Peter, I launched into another round of cold calling. I needed to recruit players, people to come to the event. I did some individual calling to the few guys and gals I knew in the area who might have an absurd interest in something like blind hockey. But more importantly and more successfully, I started calling every blind organization in the D.C. metro area: the Virginia Department for the Blind, the National Federation for the Blind, the Blinded Veterans Association, the Columbia Lighthouse for the Blind. I asked them to help put out a notice that this unique event would be happening. The D.C. Blind Sports Association put out a notice through their channels too. This group mainly organized a sport called Goalball. I cut a deal with them that if they would promote hockey then I would promote Goalball at my event, and they saw it as an opportunity—mutually beneficial. Two offerings for the same sport-interested blind demographic.

Then I hit paydirt when an eye doctor who had heard of my efforts through one of these organizations reached out to me. Her name was Tina Butera. She considered herself a huge Caps fan and she knew a lot of people in the hockey community because her ex had been a coach and she was a pediatric ophthalmologist who had treated hundreds of blind D.C. kids, some of whom she believed would cherish an opportunity to try something like Blind Hockey. She became critical both to finding players and to getting the event organized. She did at least half the leg work setting up our first Try Blind Hockey event, even using her own money to make swag—stuff like T-shirts, a banner with our Wheelers team logo on it, gift bags—and even buy pizzas afterward. It was a good lesson for me, the lift that just one motivated believer can give to such an effort.

At this same time I also learned about a charitable organization called Leveling the Playing Field. It didn't work solely with the blind, but we fit within its mandate. And, as I mentioned, to comply with USA Hockey guidelines, we had a critical need to come up with lots of fairly expensive gear. I called this organization and asked for a donation. They said they would support our effort, but they needed to know how many people would be involved. I told them, just as I told Peter Robinson, my standard answer: *I don't know yet. I'm working on recruiting. I'll get back to you.*

Thanks to all these efforts, the number of first-time skaters who signed up for the event grew and grew and kept on growing, almost magically, starting at what I thought was a respectable seven, then a couple days later eight, then 10 and then 24 before we ended up with 73 blind and visually impaired skaters signed up and ready to go.

If only we could find enough equipment!

I called Leveling the Playing Field back and told them the number of sets of equipment and they laughed at me. But they came through. They pulled it off, renting a huge box truck and showing up the day of the event with bags upon bags of helmets, shin pads, gloves, even some skates to augment what the rink's own rental program could offer us. We equipped every single person who showed up with a usable helmet and gloves. To date that initial Capitals event remains the largest Try Blind Hockey experience to have been held in the world. I hope someone beats that record, though, because I want more people to have the chance to get involved, whether as donors, volunteers, or players.

Because so many people from the Caps organization saw our turnout for the event, they knew there would be momentum for a team and, in my follow-up meeting with them, when I asked for funding, I received the equally valuable but unexpected deal to use the ice for free—albeit at that same difficult 6:00 AM timeslot.

The punchline is what came next: only about six people showed up for our first Wheelers practice. And it got worse from there. Sometimes, in those first difficult days starting the program, it would be just me and a goalie, skating together in the echoing cavern of the Caps professional hockey rink, seats upon empty seats staring down at us.

I learned pretty quickly that getting blind people to try anything once wasn't too tough. Getting them to stick with something hard could be a different matter altogether.

Chapter 8

PERSEVERANCE

Long-term success doesn't come from the exhilarating flash of inspiration. Success depends on stacking small and continual victories one atop the next.

THE STRUGGLE I EXPERIENCED converting the initial turnout from the Try Blind Hockey event into a regularly practicing team wasn't the only obstacle I had to overcome. Two others jump out as unique and informative. The first dealt with learning to help other blind people overcome their own barriers to entry for the sport. The second involved the responsibility of a founder to their creation and especially the need to reassert oneself if things start to go sideways.

The very beginning of the Wheelers program is what I call the "brick-by-brick" time period. Like I mentioned, even after the wildly successful Try Blind Hockey event we put together in February 2016, and even with the buy-in of the Washington Capitals, who donated us ice time from March until the start of the hockey season the next year—a space of about six months—we began with very low participation numbers. A few crucial volunteers also carried over from that event to the start of our practices, so we'd have about 10 people show up any given morning, with somewhere around six (or fewer) actual skaters.

We did everything we could to increase those numbers—calls, more advertising, more events—but participation wouldn't increase until I realized one key thing: most of the skaters faced some sort of personal barrier to entry to the sport.

Ice hockey—even the regulation game—isn't the easiest sport to start playing. There's a big financial investment required for skates, gear, and lessons. There is also the hurdle, if you're older, of thinking you can't skate and won't be able to learn to skate if you're not a pliable, fearless youngster. A beginner also can't just grab a ball and find any open field, like in soccer, or install a net and backboard in the driveway like with basketball. A person must find a specialized facility that maintains a sheet of ice, figure out the facility's schedule, apply to the appropriate level of skating or hockey course or league, and then probably also rearrange a lot of other life things—school, work, kids' schedules, normal life functions—to even begin the journey toward learning and enjoying the sport.

Now, layer onto this the challenges of being disabled, of needing to find a ride to the rink, of even understanding, building an awareness that something like blind hockey exists, and the challenges multiply in both number and intensity.

My goal for the program, at least that first season, focused on increasing our participation to the point where, at the end of practice, we could scrimmage five-on-five, ideally with a goalie in each net as well. This meant we needed to double the number of participants.

That very first practice when I showed up at 6:00 AM to the Capitals rink, I kept looking around, skating laps, wondering where everyone was. The taster event had so many skaters come try the sport. Even though 25 or so expressed interest in continuing, only six showed up. Less than 10 percent! I realized I had a lot of work to do and decided the only solution would be a liberal application of elbow grease.

I began to call participants from the initial event directly. If they were minors, I'd call their parents. Generally speaking, at the beginner level in both regulation and blind hockey, youths outnumber adults by two to one. This is good, because it ensures an upswell of young people who will potentially play the sport for a long time. It's also beneficial in terms of fundraising, as no one is particularly interested in donating to a 40-year-old blind man, but blind kids certainly get donor support, as they should. The mechanics of it are, however, a bit ironic because blind adults end up with more limited career prospects and tend to need more support than blind kids, who usually have parents with normal incomes.

In support of each of these populations—adult learners and the parents of blind kids who wanted to play—I began to work one-on-one to address their personal barriers to entry. Did someone need a pair of skates? I'd find them, or buy them myself, and get them delivered. Did someone need a ride to practice? No problem. I worked with them to find someone with whom they'd be comfortable commuting, often blind adults riding with the parents of blind children who had already committed to the team. Did someone need to know what sort and what price point of gear to buy? I'd show up at the hockey pro shop and help them work through the multiplicity of options, clarifying what was just a nice-to-have and what would be necessary for safety and decent beginner-level performance. My primary strategy relied on overcommunication, treating individual players like my own special projects and doing whatever I needed to do to knock down the various barriers they encountered on their unique journeys into hockey.

This same effect of brick-by-brick building happens in business, just as it happened to me in blind hockey. Even if I have a good day or a good week in the business world, I'm not guaranteed a good month or good year. Long-term success doesn't come from the exhilarating flash of inspiration. It doesn't come from the wildly successful single event, like Try Blind Hockey. Success depends on stacking small, continual victories one atop the next, all aiming at a coordinated vision. I had that vision in blind hockey. I knew what I wanted—a team large enough to play actual hockey, rather than just do drills.

By the end of the summer we had it, with our average number of skaters increasing to 15 and the number of volunteers helping drive, organize, and lead the practices stabilizing around 10 or 12. Someone less personally motivated, less personally invested in blind hockey, might have simply called the players and told them, "Well, whatever issue you're having is something you'll need to overcome. We're here with ice time whenever you decide to play." That wasn't my style, though.

The brick-by-brick approach, and the personal involvement that fueled it, did not come without disadvantages. For one, it interfered with my day job. I fielded incoming calls from blind people or parents at every hour of the day, even on the job. I felt the calling to prioritize these people, and so I'd stop whatever I was doing in the office to listen and address their needs. Because this all went down during that very busy time for Akira, when we were bidding on and winning so many government contracts, the additional calls and time spent on blind hockey didn't mean I worked less. No, I just worked later in the day, often until 8:00 or 9:00 PM.

A truly Washington, D.C., anecdote from this time reinforces the craziness of my office hours. The window above my desk faced Pennsylvania Avenue a half block from the White

House—a great location for those who could enjoy the view! What I remember the most from those days was the sound of Joe Biden's motorcade. He was vice president back then and would leave the White House at 7:00 nightly, heading to the Naval Observatory, which is the residence of the VP. That's how I knew I needed to start shifting my focus to get out of the office. It was my own early, and more positive, version of the "Thanks, Biden" slogan.

At about this same time I began raising money for the blind hockey effort. I'd started traveling around the U.S., pushing the model of our Wheelers program to other professional hockey teams. (More on that later.) Between those travels and the money I was putting into the Wheelers, I'd sunk a good deal of pocket change into the sport. I was fortunate to have money like that to spend, but I realized it wouldn't be sustainable, not if I wanted to truly propagate blind hockey nationwide.

So, in another uniquely D.C. move, I dropped by the headquarters of the Department of Veterans Affairs (VA) one day. I had started a 501(c)(3) charity to help fund the Wheelers. In the process, I heard that the VA included in its labyrinthine programs an office for the support of adaptive sports. I waited my turn in the lobby of this office and ended up meeting with the head of the program, explaining to him the basic outline of blind hockey. I wasn't expecting to receive funding from them directly, only to get some advice on where to find funding. But I brought a blind-hockey puck with me, and it caused a little stir, with several people in the office joining us, hefting the puck, hearing the ball bearings jangle within.

They explained that they did, indeed, have some grants they could offer through their annual application process. So I hustled some more, getting letters of recommendation from the United States Association of Blind Athletes and from four National Hockey League teams—Colorado, Pittsburgh, Minnesota and, of course, the Washington Capitals. Since my Wheelers charity was so new, I understood it wouldn't qualify for funding of this sort. I needed to team up with a more established 501(c)(3), an organization with a track record of administering grants, so I sought out the Blinded Veterans Association (BVA) and wrote the grant applications in its name. I made two bids to the Veterans Administration, one intending to expand blind hockey nationally, the other intending to build out BVA's infrastructure to manage adaptive sport more generally. I developed the packages, the strategies, and the budgets, basically doing all the work for both applications, and we won them both, for a total of $126,000. The BVA's CEO at the time, Al Avina, recommended that I consult to help the organization hire someone for coaching as well as managing the program in its national roll-out.

This was all a great success. It did separate me by one degree from directly administering the program, but that was okay. Akira had me busy through and through. And my focus already seemed divided enough, wanting to play as well as foster the growth of the program. So I appreciated having the BVA there to backstop me administratively and serve as the final decision-maker on anything related to these two grants.

On the BVA's behalf, I began interviewing people, looking for someone with both program management experience and hockey experience who could take on the dual roles of developing a national sport as well as coaching the local Wheelers team as a springboard to getting more blind players involved across the nation. To find leads, I talked with the Washington Capitals' community development team—the pro team's amateur affiliation. Their head, Dan Jablonic, told me that while some teams in the area are purely recreational, others have paid coaches and that those coaches usually elevate the team and increase the level of competitive hockey. That made sense. I told Dan how much money I'd raised, and he laughed at me.

"The highest-paid non-Capitals coach—the highest paid non-pro coach—in D.C. is making about $15,000 a year for his work," he said.

I had a budget of about $50,000 but needed someone able to commit to growing the program nationally, not just showing up for a couple on-ice sessions a week. The first four or five people I interviewed were lacking either hockey knowledge or management experience. It seemed like the two skills rarely resided in the same human.

Then I got introduced to a man who I'm not going to name here, though he's known well-enough in the blind hockey community. Let's call him Bobby. I brought Bobby to the rink to skate with me after a first phone interview. He took the time to coach me individually, giving me a lot of pointers on how I could do better with my skating. He seemed really enthusiastic. I asked the BVA to do a background check on him and then I recommended him based on my observations of him during our ice time.

Unfortunately, the BVA did not follow through on the background check. Instead, the organization took my recommendation as enough of a guarantee and simply offered him a contract sight unseen. I found out shortly after this that our new coach and program manager, this Bobby, had been banned from coaching at the rink where we had ice because he and his wife owned a promotional modeling business and kept approaching the Capitals' Ice Girls, the on-ice version of cheerleaders, to do promotional modeling on the side.

The Caps had received numerous complaints about Bobby's business practices.

However, the general manager of the Caps' rink decided to make an exception to Bobby's ban because he was working to support our charity. Bobby then proceeded to use his first organizing event in February 2017—one year after my highly successful Try Blind Hockey event—to bring in several Trump appointees to put on a political spectacle, using disabled people to show that "Republicans have hearts too." It became very clear very quickly that Bobby had only taken the job with the BVA in order to publicize himself and create a platform to support his other interests and business ventures.

Per his contract, Bobby tried to recruit veterans to play blind hockey. He didn't succeed, though. Not a single new blind hockey player joined our ranks due to his efforts. A few signed up with him to take pictures on the ice and he helped them skate a bit. But, more concerning, he also simultaneously seemed to be on the lookout for the more gullible types and would enlist them in another scheme of his—an idea he was pushing to establish a cryptocurrency nominally designed to benefit disabled people. Now, cryptocurrency bros have deservedly created a bad name for themselves. They're like the bro equivalent of the Lululemon yoga set—lots of show, lots of talk, not much commitment to basic principles. And this guy was the worst of them.

As part of our obligations in support of the VA grant contract, we'd set goals for how much recruitment was supposed to occur. Grant money would flow to the BVA from the VA according to our effort's success with these milestones. We also owed the VA regular reporting on the progress of blind hockey nationally. About five months into this, I discovered not only that Bobby wasn't writing or submitting reports, but also that of the 70 or so veterans we'd set as a target for enrollment nationally, this guy had found only five who would even try skating, let alone suit up for hockey. He hosted failed event after failed event and eventually started approaching individual players on the Washington D.C. team to ask them if they'd be willing to help him start his own team in the D.C. area, basically trying to split our Wheelers team in two, because he didn't like the questions I had begun asking him.

Canada had hired this wonderful man, Matt Morrow, to build its program nationally—the same guy who had picked me up from the train station when I went to the first blind hockey event in Newburgh a year and a half earlier. Everyone involved with the Wheelers reflected on Canada's success with Matt, and it became a bit of a rallying cry, that we needed to find our own Matt.

Bobby's failures ramified. It wasn't just incompetence. I feared I'd made an even graver mistake, recommending a scam artist to the BVA. None of the goals we'd set for our program were going to be achieved because Bobby wasn't interested in growing the blind hockey program, but in launching a cryptocurrency or pursuing whatever other goals he had set for his side businesses.

The tipping point happened during a multi-day event we held in D.C. Bobby had organized it, with players coming in from out of town to play at the Capitals' rink, and he didn't even bother to show up for practice on the second day. By this point we had more than 200 volunteers across the U.S. who had participated in our events and supported blind hockey one way or another, trying to get blind athletes on the ice. To this day, the only one who has ever made a dime off blind hockey has been this man, Bobby. He was supposed to be organizing and growing the game, and he didn't show up for half of the event.

I made the decision in my mind right then and there that he wasn't going to keep running my 501(c)(3), which was not the same thing as BVA's grant-funded nationwide program. I did consult with them, and I recommended they let him go at the same time as I removed him from coaching the Wheelers, but he told them some sort of sob story to justify why they should keep him around.

I arrived a few short days later to the locker room of one of our local Washington Wheelers practices carrying a poster, with the Wheelers logo on it, and I asked all the players at the session that morning to sign it. A couple of the volunteers and I mounted the poster in a frame. It said, in big letters, "Thank you Bobby." I let this guy coach his last practice. Then, having coordinated all this with a few of the volunteers who I knew also wanted him gone, I went to the locker room, got the poster, skated it out onto the ice and handed it to him at the end of practice. As nice as pie, I told him we wanted to thank him for all the work he'd done for the Washington Wheelers and for blind hockey. But I added the stinger of also being very clear that this would be his last practice with the team. If the BVA wanted to keep him around, that was its business, but I wasn't going to let him continue to tank the charity I'd started.

Now, Bobby had been at least somewhat clever. In his process of searching for the more gullible members of the blind community to support his cryptocurrency effort, and in conjunction with his Trumpism, he'd tried to drive a wedge between the parents on the team by identifying a few more right-wing, religious-minded parents and preying on them. This crew he convinced to briefly separate from the Wheelers and attempt to set up their own team, while also trying to commandeer our ice time. If we had lost that free ice time, donated by the Capitals, we would have lost the team as a whole. But I managed to convince enough of the other parents, those who could see through Bobby's scams, to start coaching our practices ourselves again. We went back to a volunteer model, rather than relying on a paid coach. This was a tough pill to swallow, after all the effort put into raising funds.

But the parents stepped up. Five of them went on to get their USA Hockey coaching certificates, just as I had done.

The BVA eventually lost its grant from Veterans Affairs. And, in consequence, it eventually fired Bobby, who was never again to be seen in or around blind hockey, though he is still trying to launch a cryptocurrency that somehow leverages his association with adaptive sports. My take on him—though I've never been privy to his accounting—is that he's just a run-of-the-mill con artist, as have been so many people trying to operate in and take advantage of the crypto craze. With both the more religious faction of parents and the few blind people he recruited to support his crypto efforts, he seemed simply to be trading on the exposure and platform that came from his association with blind hockey, trying his darndest to make a quick buck.

In the same way, perhaps, that art imitates life and life imitates art, my company, Akira, underwent a similar inflection point at this same time.

We'd been doing great, bidding on a plethora of government contracts and winning 17 of them. This represented huge growth for a new company in the government contracting space. But much like the one wrong step we took with blind hockey, hiring a borderline con artist, so too did we misstep with one of our new government contracts.

Akira's strategy focused on taking some risks, underbidding competitors in order to establish ourselves. The risk materialized when we signed a contract with the U.S. Army's Dugway Proving Grounds outside Salt Lake City.

Now, Salt Lake City seems like it should be relatively harmless. A peaceful and well-mannered corner of the United States, filled with Mormons and ski resorts, right?

Well, what attracted the U.S. Army to this location was something else entirely: the remote, austere environment of the salt flats in the desert. Our contract—which involved upgrading all the wired and wireless networks for the Army's facilities in this location—came with some challenges we did not anticipate from the urbanity of our D.C. metropolis.

I experienced this firsthand. Showing up there one day, just as I had done to several other military-related kick-off meetings, I planned to Uber to the front gate of the base and then walk to the building where I would meet with the Proving Grounds' IT department.

No dice.

I couldn't find an Uber driver willing to drive all that way into the desert. I was stranded and forced to pay a taxi driver $500 not only to take me out to the base, but also to wait around all day for me. What's more, I had to argue with the guards at the facility's gates to allow my driver on base. He didn't have the necessary clearances or permissions, but the building where my meeting was scheduled happened to be 18 miles from the gate. Not walkable. I showed them my blind cane. I had entrance credentials and eventually talked them into allowing my taxi driver to take me to the meeting, which was no small feat.

We had participated in multiple calls with the Dugway teams, preparatory to bidding, in order to ensure we filed the lowest bid and won the contract. Never had we thought to ask about the distances between facilities. This 18-mile drive turned out to be no small anomaly. Everything at Dugway seemed to be separated by miles and miles of dusty, salty nothingness.

What's more, the local IT personnel in Salt Lake City knew this. That's really why we won the bid. None of them would deign to work for us, not at the rates we'd quoted Dugway. All the IT people knew what work at Dugway meant, including not just the harsh conditions and long drives, but also potential exposure to aftereffects from whatever experiments the Army had conducted there over the decades. We based the numbers in our bid on one particular local IT guru who claimed to know all the Verizon service personnel in the area who were willing to do side gigs and thereby form a ready-made workforce for the contract. In a clear analogy with Bobby, my sociopathic coach for the Wheelers, when it came time to organize the teams to do this work, this local guru suddenly doubled his prices.

We couldn't perform the work at such a huge loss. Yet, if ever a company backs out on a government contract, it faces the possibility of receiving a Contractor Performance Assessment Review (CPAR), also known as the kiss of death, which at this delicate stage in Akira's growth would have ended the possibility of future government work.

We withdrew from the contract, pleading ignorance of the distances and difficulties involved. Fortunately, Dugway did not file the CPAR paperwork, and we ended up with what's called "Termination for Convenience"—allowing us to continue doing government business.

The two experiences—with the Wheelers and with the Dugway contract—made me realize that if you mess up, you have to admit your mistake quickly or you might lose the whole thing. Perhaps more importantly, given my central role in both episodes, I also realized that a founder or creator bears a responsibility that lingers long after the moment of initiation. People depend on the work a founder does. They rely on and expect a certain amount of future direction, guidance and staying power. If you go out into the world and create something, an obligation ensues not only to see it to a point of stability, or put it to rest, but also to step back in, as I had to do with the Wheelers, if something starts to go off track.

I often think about all the people the $126,000 in grant money could have helped, all the skates it could have purchased, all the ice time or plane tickets to adaptive sporting events, if we'd found someone capable to administer the program, rather than just someone interested in ringing a cash register for his own benefit. I bet there are dozens of potential blind hockey players we never found because of this episode.

Not that I'm in any way equivalent to Steve Jobs, but he had to do the same thing with Apple at a critical juncture.

Around this same time, USA Hockey's disabled division was having trouble with ongoing allegations of misconduct. Understandably, the adaptive sports community developed a heightened awareness and sensitivity to perceived inappropriate actions. Using this in one last futile attempt to tip the scales in his favor, Bobby spread rumors that somehow my team and I had committed a SafeSport violation, when no such action or even perception actually existed. Quite to the contrary—rather than trying to achieve any individual financial benefit from blind hockey, I had raised significant amounts of grant funding for the sport, which was paying Bobby's salary at the time and none of which I personally benefited from.

I take pride in the fact there's still a thriving blind hockey team in D.C., all because a couple of volunteer parents and I had the guts to take this guy on, take the team back, and right the ship. Six years later the Wheelers are still going strong and, from our ranks, eight players have gone on to play for the U.S. National Blind Hockey Team.

Chapter 9

ENTREPRENEURSHIP

Hoping that better players would magically show up in the Washington metro area wasn't enough. I needed to do something.

THE HEART OF ENTREPRENEURSHIP, for me, revolves around taking a calculated risk and then convincing others to take that risk with you. When you launch a start-up business, if you're just an army of one, then you amount to not much more than an independent contractor, whether you're working as a dentist, a consultant, or a lawyer. You have skills in a particular field. And you have the dream to do that work yourself, at least to start and to a certain degree of effort. The big differentiator is that, no matter what the particular field of work may be, you go beyond just doing the job yourself and you start to bring others along with you on that journey.

When I joined a sport that was being made up as I went along, no good videos existed on YouTube. No handbook had been produced. No roadmap had been charted for the *how* behind starting not just a team but a sport overall. None of the NHL teams I approached or the blind players I recruited into the sport initially even thought it was a good idea, this concept of blind hockey, let alone something that should be considered safe, fun, or fulfilling. Trying to get someone to believe in something that doesn't yet exist, at least not in the form that they'll enjoy it most—that's what entrepreneurs have to do, whether starting a company, a sports team, or a book club in your neighborhood. It might just be you and a couple of girlfriends drinking wine for the first few meetings of the club. Not everyone will show up having read *Pride and Prejudice,* cover to cover, and be ready to talk about it. The entrepreneur must sell that vision for a long time before it becomes real.

Bringing an entrepreneurial mindset to both my work and to blind hockey has served me well. This model, as I see it, has four parts: (1) having a vision, (2) building a model, (3) refining the model, and (4) replicating the model. Strangely enough, this exact process played out in 2016 simultaneously both in my business life and in a push I made to bring blind hockey to other locations across the United States.

Two things motivated me to look beyond D.C. for blind hockey, to really grow the game and not just grow a local team.

First, while building the Wheelers via that brick-by-brick, player-by-player approach, and after we had recruited at least enough players of sufficient quality to skate cross-ice in a three-on-three (rather than the normal full-ice, five-on-five hockey format), the legwork I'd put in and the lack of additional players joining our Wheelers practices made it clear to me that D.C. just didn't have enough blind skaters to develop a mature league on its own. In truth, I was never trying to build a league. But the players who were practicing hard didn't have enough people to compete against. At least the Canadians had their national tournament. As our practices grew more familiar and as our skills solidified in D.C., we needed the prospect of competition to motivate us.

When thinking about the search for good blind players, I like to use the analogy of trying to find a needle in a haystack within an even bigger haystack. What I mean by that is that if a blind player who is already really good at hockey is the needle, then the first haystack is the sum total of all the blind people in a region. Across North America, only about 1 percent of the population is legally blind. Those are bad odds, for sure. Yet the second haystack makes it even tougher, as the type and timing of the onset of blindness creates an outsized influence. Did blindness begin after learning to play hockey at some level, yet also before the person got too old to play competitively? Finding a player in this Goldilocks zone, in the age window where they might be or become an effective blind hockey player, just turns out to be a numbers game. I figured this equation out pretty quickly while trying to overcome the recruiting hurdle for the Wheelers. Even though I'd gotten 73 blind people to turn out for our Try Blind Hockey event, only three of them had ever touched a hockey puck before that event and none of them had played competitively.

I realized that another extenuating issue factored in for the Wheelers. While the successes of the Capitals, who went to the Stanley Cup Final in 1998 and were gearing up for another run in 2016—eventually winning it in 2018—created keen interest in regulation hockey, that interest requires a generation or two in order to foster deeply rooted local youth programs. D.C., being south of the Mason-Dixon Line, just didn't have the same history with ice hockey as more northern states like Minnesota, Maine, or Massachusetts. So the number of potential players in D.C. thinned even more as a result, with players my age or older not having grown up with robust ice hockey programs, either to watch as fans or to skate in as youth. In short, D.C. could barely support the Wheelers, with a tremendous amount of brick-by-brick effort required to turn skaters out.

This leads to point number two in my motivation for starting to franchise the Wheelers' blind hockey model.

In March 2016, even before doing all the work to submit the BVA grant applications and go down the disastrous road of hiring Bobby as our program manager and coach, I got invited to participate in Canada's National Blind Hockey Tournament. Before this tournament, my experience playing blind hockey had been confined to D.C., though I knew there were really good Canadian players. However, in D.C. I found myself dominating the play, and this led me to believe I'd become pretty good at the sport. I developed a false sense of confidence. While we were all trying hard to improve on the Wheelers, our second-best player was, for example, a 15-year-old blind girl who had played some travel hockey in the far suburbs of Northern Virginia. Other assorted blind players then taking the ice during our Wheelers practices were really old and had played long ago or really young and just beginning to learn the game.

All that said, I went to Canada and had my eyes opened for me. There were at least 30 Canadian blind players way better than me. They competed in a Select level of the tournament, whereas I slotted into their paradigm one level lower, in the Intermediate/Open division. Watching the Select players in this tournament made me wonder if there were skaters in America just as good as some of these Canadians who simply hadn't heard about blind hockey yet.

The combination of these things, of realizing that D.C. just wasn't a big enough haystack and that I dearly wanted to play, in the United States, at a similarly competitive level as the Canadians, gave me the motivation to grow the game in America. If I ever wanted to see blind hockey become a real sport in the United States, if I ever wanted to participate in that sport at a higher level myself, I had to help build the whole game, not just a single D.C. team. Hoping that better players would magically show up in the Washington metro area wasn't enough. I needed to do something.

I had identified a gap in the model of what I was trying to do in blind hockey. And I decided to fill it. That is the spirit of the entrepreneur. And it's also what I happened to be doing with Akira in my business career at just that same moment.

We'd grown Akira from $3.5 million in annual revenue when I first joined to more than $110 million by the time that year's sprint of submitting for those many dozens of government contracts finished. As that process unfolded I saw firsthand several gaps in the way that companies like Akira approach government contracting, along with several opportunities. One of those opportunities is that service-disabled, veteran-owned businesses get a leg-up as they start in this field. I decided to grow in that direction and, by the middle of 2016, right at the same time as I began to work on franchising the model of the Wheelers to other locations that might be ripe for blind hockey, I also made the decision to leave Akira and start my own company.

The exit from Akira didn't happen immediately, and that was great. I had time to leave the company in good shape, with the full support and blessing of my two primary business partners. That change, though I started thinking through it and preparing for it in mid-2016, wouldn't happen until early 2017.

In the meantime, I got busy again with blind hockey.

I first helped put together a Try Blind Hockey event in Pittsburgh, under the auspices of the city's pro team, the Penguins. Matt Morrow, the head of Canadian Blind Hockey, had asked me to get involved with that. Matt is such a class act and his purpose and mine aligned so closely that it was a no-brainer to go up there. Plus, Pittsburgh is only four hours from D.C.

By this time, the Washington Capitals had risen to become a close second to the Colorado Avalanche in my love for professional hockey. Pittsburgh had knocked out the Caps on its way to winning the first of back-to-back Stanley Cups in 2016 and 2017. The Try Blind Hockey event happened to coincide with the Penguins' Stanley Cup parade, so I crossed paths with a couple of Penguins players—Phil Kessel and Patrick Hornqvist, who were still "giddy" from their Stanley Cup parade experience—as I tried to shepherd blind kids into the arena.

I also began, late in the summer of 2016, to make contact with the Colorado Avalanche. Of course they were on my radar, as I'd been such a longtime fan. The Avalanche started out a bit hesitant about getting involved in blind hockey, so I asked Pete Robinson, the Head of Public Relations for the Capitals who had been such a great ally, to reach out and vouch for me and for the proposed event.

Minnesota became the fourth location I pursued. Looking at a map, and thinking through the history of hockey in the United States, I knew that if good blind hockey players would be hiding anywhere, it'd be most likely in the far northern states. Minnesota has a great hockey tradition, so the odds of finding a few players who grew up skating and stickhandling but then went blind were higher than elsewhere. I began reaching out to various people in Minnesota, sending them my organizing documents for the Wheelers, and I didn't really have to do much else there. Blind hockey took off on its own, with homegrown support and leadership and with the Minnesota Wild—the NHL team that filled the gap of the long-departed North Stars in 2000—lending their full weight to the project. The USA Disabled Hockey representative for the region, a woman named Toni, ran with the programs, implementing everything based on the documents I sent. It was very satisfying to see them pull off a great Try Blind Hockey event later that year and to do so without me having to go there in person.

Other teams held similar events in Philadelphia and Carolina over the next year or two, and I helped with the event in St. Louis. As I was working with the Avalanche, Bobby and I together reached out to the Blues, hosting their event one day after Colorado hosted its event. They were also the first two teams that used their actual pro arenas to host the events. During this time Hartford, Connecticut, began its own foray into blind hockey independently from any of my efforts, solely based on local organizers' grassroots mobilization. I eventually lent them a bit of an assist with the 501(c)(3) process and organizing their business, but Hartford's team came about due to a few blind people who were already getting together to skate just as friends.

A convergence between these activities and my business entrepreneurship began to take shape in January 2017. My exit from Akira had become official, and I used the proceeds to found my own government contracting business, which I called Cosain—a word that means "to defend and protect" in Gaelic. I couldn't have made this leap without the full support of my former partners at Akira, and I'll always be grateful to Srini Chennamaraja, Akira's CEO, for giving me my first chance to be the COO of a fledgling start-up. He played a key role in encouraging me to start a franchise of my own, a little version of Akira, at just this same time when I had begun franchising the Wheelers' model of blind hockey.

It's a scary moment, launching a company of your own.

And that first contract in Colorado wasn't yet even a glimmer in my imagination when I left Akira.

That January I took an office on Capitol Hill, a block from a homeless shelter. I walked my blind self over to that office, picked up the key from my new landlord, opened a small, two-desk room, and got to work, with no one else to keep me company in that gray, quiet space. I realized pretty quickly I'd need to hire at least one other person, both because I needed to round out my skill set for pursuing certain technology contracts and because, as an extrovert, I just couldn't sit alone all day in front of a computer and phone. With Srini's blessing, I brought over a promising systems engineering graduate who had recently started working with Akira. I recruited her and we started writing proposals to let various federal agencies know that we were available. Then I spent the majority of 2017 on planes, splitting my time between office calls with potential customers and the equally invigorating work helping kickstart blind hockey franchises.

Around this same time, I took a dirty hit on the ice while playing sighted hockey and broke my fibula. This was during the lead-up to again competing in the Canadian Blind Hockey Tournament, but this time at the Elite/Select level. I'd been notified of that selection in January 2017 and suffered my injury less than two weeks later. That was a huge deal, as neither the U.S. nor Canada had representative teams yet. So this was, for me, the equivalent of making a national team. I wanted to play on this team so badly that I took a very aggressive stance with the orthopedic doctors I saw. I wanted to be back on the ice with a passion. And so I basically strong-armed them into putting a titanium plate in my ankle to reinforce it and allow me to get on the ice faster.

In retrospect, this has caused a lot of issues for me—my ankle and lower leg still aren't the same. Yet it also, ultimately, facilitated the best moment, the high point of my athletics career, my proudest physical accomplishment. I have the gold medal from that competition on the wall in my office even now. I scored a goal in the championship game essentially on one leg. Competing in that state, not just blind but also hobbled, was harder than the bit of boxing I'd done at the military academy, harder than anything I was made to do in basic training, harder than anything I undertook while playing for Team USA against Canada.

Throughout all of this, a constant thorn in my side was the situation with the Wheelers and our con-artist coach and program manager. I was doing everything I could to franchise and build blind hockey, while he was not only doing nothing but also draining resources and time.

It wasn't all bad, though—far from it.

The highlight of that year for me ended up being the Try Blind Hockey event we put together with the Avalanche. I'd of course been an Avalanche fan all through the years, continuing to follow them even as I also began to root for the Caps in D.C. This event hit a real personal note for me, as their arena—at that time called the Pepsi Center—happened to have been the last place I saw a live sporting event with my own two eyes, the Detroit Red Wings versus the Avalanche on St. Patrick's Day in 2001. It's still the happiest place for me in sport. The Avs giving me that building for one day in order to bring a bunch of blind people onto the ice, helping them do something I loved, goes down as one of the best days of my life.

By the end of 2017, I had found seven or eight other pretty capable blind hockey players spread across the U.S., close to but perhaps not quite playing at the rarified level of the Canadian Select Blind Hockey players. A couple of these players hailed from Colorado.

This is where the convergence between my business and blind hockey really began to show itself. I started seeking contract work with Cosain in Colorado. That next December, almost a year after launching Cosain, I landed a project with a pharmacogenetics lab in downtown Denver, providing them with IT services and product development support. I had just begun a relationship in D.C. but decided, even with the pressure of leaving behind a love interest, I would sign myself up to go to Denver for the duration of this six-month contract, from January to June of 2018.

The backstory of my relationship ties into hockey in a distinct way as well. This was a pretty serious relationship, going for over a year by the time I left for Denver. We'd met three days after the surgery to repair my ankle. My doctor told me I could put weight on it as tolerated, and I can tolerate a lot. So, there I was—if you'll imagine it—hopped up on Percocet, and making the further bad decision to join a few of my friends at a local wine bar. A woman in the group noticed me reading the wine menu upside down. At first she just thought I was drunk and high, because, being the stubborn guy I am, I'd not arrived using my blind cane. This woman and I got talking. She turned out to be an orthopedic physician's assistant, so we had a lot to discuss that evening, given the state of my ankle and my intent to immediately continue skating on it competitively. The relationship kicked off from that very moment.

Although we ended up being off-again, on-again—especially during my time in Denver when I visited her in D.C. a few times and she traveled to see me once or twice—and although she was against the idea of me continuing to pursue competitive hockey, thinking it got in the way of our relationship, she did help me prepare for tournaments by shooting up my ankle or knees with an anesthetic or an anti-inflammatory. Definitely a nice perk of that affair.

This relationship also influenced my future to some degree, as the situation mirrored one I would experience again, two years later. Then, rather than trying to keep the relationship going when I went away to support the eventual contract I'd take in Louisiana, I broke it off. And that almost ended up being the biggest mistake of all! But more about that later. I made a relationship decision later in life because of my experience going back and forth from Denver. I felt like I wasn't able to be fair to the relationship while simultaneously training for hockey and working really long hours for work. The relationship itself didn't get in the way of anything; I just wasn't able to prioritize it. And, when it came to that similar situation with the Louisiana contract, I didn't feel like I wanted that to happen again. Whew, I got lucky during the Louisiana contract though—or else I wouldn't be in the perfect marriage I am now!

But that story is for a later chapter. Now, going back to the timeline of this story: I moved from D.C. to Denver and took up this contracted position in pharmacogenetics, renting an apartment in downtown Denver, and worked the contract while skating three mornings a week with the other good blind players I'd found. We did this at just as painfully an early hour as I'd gotten used to on Capitals' sheet of ice, albeit now at the University of Denver's Magnus Arena.

My typical day over this six-month stretch had a sense of military regularity to it: 6:00 AM ice time, followed by an immediate trek to the pharmacogenetics laboratory. They thankfully had a shower, so I'd show up there with my gear, get myself into shape (and scent) for a full day in the office, lay my sweaty gear out to dry in the parking lot of the lab, start work around 8:30 AM, work all day building this really cool technology product to help diagnose underlying genetic conditions that would cause people to not metabolize certain medications, then go back to my apartment solo, throw my gear in one corner of the rented room, perhaps work out after work, and then re-attack my other pet project—helping build and franchise more blind hockey opportunities around the United States.

To cap this off, just after I landed in Denver, I found out that USA Hockey would field a U.S. National Blind Hockey Team in 2018. Everything conspired to point me in that direction. I was in Denver, at altitude, the perfect place to train. I'd found the best set of U.S. blind players I'd yet encountered. I had regular ice time. So I figured it was the perfect opportunity, and I committed my heart, mind, and body to prepare myself to try out for the team.

Chapter 10

CHALLENGE

I'm a team sport kind of guy, and I found that being a small business founder didn't satisfy me or keep me on track. I felt much more fulfilled by hockey.

BEFORE JUMPING INTO THE STORY of my time with Team USA, though, Canadian blind hockey and my involvement with it deserves more attention.

Hockey, no matter which version of the sport, just tends to be better north of the border, in the land of "Ya Hey" and "Hoser." It's their national game, after all. By playing in a number of tournaments across Canada—the first being in Toronto in 2016, but then later in Ottawa, Vancouver, Edmonton, and again in Toronto—I went to the source of hockey, really the epicenter of it, and got to experience play at a level that wasn't available down south.

The math (as I've mentioned a few times and in various contexts) in blind hockey is simple—there are only about 500 people in the world who play it with any regularity right now. Of the 50 best players in North America, I'd say 40 of them are in Canada, and 10 are in the States—so either you're playing watered-down blind hockey in Pittsburgh or Chicago or you're flying north of the border. At this time, already 40 years old, I could afford to fly out and participate in nearly every Canadian tournament. The discriminator for me wasn't so much the cost, but the timing, whether it fit in my work schedule. As a result of all these tournaments, I developed meaningful friendships with a lot of my Canadian counterparts.

The top trophy in blind hockey is the Courage Cup, awarded to the winner of the Canadian National Blind Hockey Tournament. Each year it occurs in March, with teams falling predominantly into three levels: Beginner/Extremely Low Vision, Open/Intermediate, or Select/Advanced. As I previously mentioned, the first year I competed in the Courage Cup tournament I did so in the Open level, which as one of the better players in the United States opened my eyes to how much I still had to learn about hockey. I definitely wasn't one of the better players in Canada!

The winning team of the highest division gets its name engraved on the Courage Cup, just as the winning team in the NHL ends up on the Stanley Cup. (The names for the divisions have changed from time to time as the sport grows, so it's not always been the Select or Advanced Division, but it's always been the team from the highest division of that particular year that claims the actual Cup.)

The name of the Courage Cup comes with its own interesting backstory.

In 2013, my friend and one of my heroes, Mark Demontis, decided to try to raise money to start a blind hockey charity for Canada. To help publicize this effort, he hit upon the idea of rollerblading from Toronto to Vancouver, making a lot of headlines along the way as a blind man rollerblading across the country, and raised $100,000 Canadian dollars.

Mark, like me, is an entrepreneur when it comes to blind hockey. Canada didn't have a unified blind hockey system until Mark raised enough money to start a national-level program. Mark recognized that if the blind hockey being played in Toronto and Montreal was ever going to expand to the rest of Canada, then significant investment was needed. Mark was well-situated to lead this charge. He had grown up playing hockey at a high level, even earning an AAA contract. But as he graduated out of the Bantam Youth leagues as one of the better players and started to prepare to go to the United States to play in college, he was diagnosed with Leber's disease. Leber's is similar to the Stargardt disease that I have. It's a rare retinal condition that can result in more central vision loss even than Stargardt if it is bad. Like me, Mark is considered a B2 on the International Blind Sports Federation's scale of blindness, almost completely blind but retaining some peripheral vision. In short, Mark went from a promising hockey career to newly diagnosed blindness, yet he still wanted to play hockey.

Mark became my inspiration for trying to scale a national program. He and I worked closely together as I helped start the D.C. program. He even came to D.C. for my organizing event and helped lead it, along with Matt Morrow, whom he had hired to lead Canadian Blind Hockey with the proceeds of his rollerblade-across-Canada fundraiser. Both Mark and Matt are about 10 years younger than me. They're also the first two people who are younger than me that I consider mentors.

I got to know them the night after the first blind hockey event I went to in Newburgh in 2015, that trip I mentioned where I first partied in NYC for Halloween, then took the train up the Hudson Valley early the next morning. Matt was the one who picked me up from the train station that day when I realized Uber wouldn't be an option in Newburgh. After the event finished, Mark and Matt invited me to accompany them back to Manhattan for a follow-on blind sports conference. I ended up talking for hours with them on a balcony of the Standard Hotel. Mark shared with me his vision for blind hockey, growing it into a Paralympic sport. It lit a fire in me and was the very moment when I decided to start a program in D.C. I figured if Mark could rollerblade all the way across Canada to raise money, the least I could do would be to put my back into trying to grow a program in D.C.

Mark has been a hockey mentor to me, and I've been a life mentor to him.

He lost his vision before he turned 17. That's such a pivotal time in a young man's life, with so many milestones happening during those years. He found himself scared of what life might hold for him, losing a scholarship, trying to figure out what sort of life he was going to lead after losing his vision. Compared to him, I had been given a chance to finish college and jumpstart my career before being diagnosed with Stargardt disease. Mark really inspired me and taught me on the hockey rink—I'd reach out to him and ask him about how he thought about things on the ice, what he would do in certain situations, how he'd react to various on-ice scenarios. He was (and still is) a great player. Even blind, even using the big, heavy blind-hockey puck, he can probably score a "Michigan" goal—which involves using the blade of a stick a bit like a spoon, picking the puck up, carrying it almost levitating above the ice, and flipping it into the goal. Such a maneuver requires years of practice and finely honed small motor skills in the wrists, as well as finely tuned balance while skating, and is not something a novice undertakes.

Mark and I were linemates on my last Canadian team in 2022. So I enjoyed the sense of symmetry there, with Mark representing both my first encounter with blind hockey at Newburgh and one of my last competitive hockey experiences.

In addition to hiring Matt Morrow to lead blind hockey in Canada, Mark used the money he'd raised to start a charity called Courage Canada, which in 2013 hosted the first true National Championship for blind hockey and the winners got their names inscribed on the brand-new Courage Cup.

By the time I first played in the competition in 2016, it had expanded to two divisions: Open and Select. Although I was one of the better players in the second tier, I set a goal to make it into the elite Select Division by 2017 so that I could have a chance at hoisting the Courage Cup.

Like a lot of professional players who play forward, I typically take the center position on weaker teams. Center is the lynchpin for the attacking side of the ice. The center handles face-offs, which is when the referee drops the puck to start play. Strategy at most face-offs involves the center trying to win the puck and usually, but not always, pull it back to his or her own defensemen in order to set up a play. Centers also generally roam free, from one side of the ice to the other, whereas the wings on each side, called the right and left wings, usually stay on their own sides of the ice. Right wings are typically right-handed (so their dominant hand is along the boards, allowing them to catch passes and maneuver in tight situations better), whereas left wings are usually the left-handed shooters. The more advanced the play becomes, the more fluid these definitions of positional play end up. Sometimes skaters choose to play on the side opposite their dominant hand, confident they can do well against the boards in any situation and preferring to shoot closer to the center of the ice, where the angles are better. It starts to get both very technical and very much a matter of preference and of how the team itself, and its players, measure up and interact best with one another.

But for beginners, the concept of left-handed on left side, right-handed on right side, and best skater in the center makes understanding the positions easier. As a result, at beginner and even Open/Intermediate levels, the best player is usually the center. Defensemen are usually bigger and slower than forwards; as a result they have their own metrics of comparative value and can often be the best player on the ice at any given time, though usually not the speediest. Wings tend to be less experienced or skilled than the center, but not always. Sometimes a wing just happens to be very good from one side of the ice, better than from the other, and therefore the speed and value of the skater on that side of the ice means they'll line up there, even if they're somewhat better overall than the center.

Because, at least in the United States, I usually profiled as one of the stronger skaters, I therefore often played center on U.S. teams. In Canadian play, the situation would reverse itself and I'd end up skating on the wing in stronger teams. As one of my Canadian teammates put it, "Compared to actual good Canadian players, you skate like you've got two broken ankles." (Note: This wasn't too far from the truth at the time! I had indeed broken one ankle and had rushed my recovery in order to be on the ice. So I didn't feel too bad about the jibe.)

Throughout 2017 I played all over both the U.S. and Canada, and I figured out what kind of player I was at a truly competitive level: still that same sort of "try hard" athlete who could skate fairly fast in a straight line, score some goals, and backcheck my ass off. I wasn't fancy, especially compared to someone like Mark Demontis. I wasn't always smooth. But I gave it my all, every second on the ice and in the locker room.

This was a year in which I really caught up to other players who'd been playing hockey for most of their lives, hitting my stride as a skater.

First, a competition hosted in Edmonton over Thanksgiving, called the Western Regional Blind Hockey Tournament (but with many of the same skaters making the trip out to the event, scrambling onto teams, all of us assembled from the grand total of 300 or so players in both countries who regularly competed.) This was the best tournament I ever played. I think I contributed 10 or 11 points over the four games we played. I thought we would win the tournament too. But in the final game, we lost 11–10 on the final shift, thanks to this kid who came out of nowhere to play in his first blind hockey tournament.

We had started the Edmonton tourney, beginning on the Thursday before the weekend's play, with our usual "leveling game"—designed to let us assess skill levels, especially if a lot of unknown players had come to participate. This helps fairly distribute talent across teams for the weekend's play. Again: blind hockey is not big enough yet for cities to play each other, so most really competitive tournaments continue to adhere to the scramble format.

One kid in particular, on the team I played against that Thursday, lit everyone up. I was in the locker room after the game, having my typical post-game beverage, when Matt Morrow—the director of the tournament—came into the locker room and said: "Hey Craig, pack up your shit, you've been traded."

I was a little confused, but gathered my gear and started to head to my new team's locker room, when this tall, lanky kid walked past me in the hallway between the locker rooms and said, "Great game, Craig. Man, I'm not looking forward to playing you tomorrow."

The kid who said that turned out to be Jason Yuha, the guy who had dominated play during our leveling scrimmage. We call him the Wayne Gretzky of blind hockey now because he's clearly the best player on any team when he skates.

Moral of the story: if you're ever faced with a trivia question asking, "Who got traded for the best blind hockey player in the world after his first game?" the answer is, yours truly, Craig Fitzpatrick.

Second anecdote from those days: in addition to doing a lot of good work trying to stand up blind hockey teams across the U.S., I'd be remiss to not mention that I retained some of my hoodlum ways, the same flair for extroverted adventures that had served me so well in Dubai and elsewhere. (But that had, I think, begun to grow a bit tamer by 2017, as the grace of aging into my forties settled around me.) When not working with blind kids, and after a couple of drinks, you could still see the temptation to revert to my degenerate ways.

Here's a tasty morsel to memorialize this.

Part of the allure of blind hockey for a lot of people is that we get to hang out with other people who "get us'" for a weekend, and the social aspect is just as good as the hockey. A magnet for many of these social interactions has been one of our goalies, a guy from Toronto named Joey "the Wall" Cabral. He's completely blind, as all goalies must be, and he works for the Toronto Police.

Joey's a popular player. Many among us who want to party after or between the games will find their way to his hotel room. On one such night, I noticed Joey often stepping outside the hotel to smoke cigarettes with a few other players. I decided to prank him. We were all blind in this partying group, and Joey was a bit tipsy to boot. So I took his TV remote control, turned on the big screen, and got my face within about an inch of it so I could see the pixelated text. I pressed the "menu" button, then scrolled to the pay-per-view section. One of the other players, who could see a little, narrated events for the rest of the room. I selected a Britney Spears concert, then turned the volume up as high as it could go before hitting play.

While the rest of the room waited for Joey to return, I went to the front desk of the hotel and asked for a roll of duct tape. I made up a lame excuse about the heater rattling and the receptionist dug a roll out of their storeroom closet. I then went back to Joey's room and duct taped the TV plug to the outlet, so he couldn't unplug it. By this point, the atmosphere in the room vacillated somewhere between groaning and howling with laughter. Not finished yet, I removed the batteries from Joey's remote. Then I hid the remote in Joey's hockey bag and put the batteries in his toiletry kit. The scene was set.

In walked Joey. He was the goalie for the team I was scheduled to play the next morning. He was three sheets to the wind, fumbling for the door, and all he heard were screaming girls and Britney Spears' voice.

Joey's initial confusion turned into laughter, and then a little anger.

"What the heck is this?" he asked. "And why's it on my TV?"

He heard laughter in response. More anger flared in his voice.

"Someone turn it off," he said. Then still more anger: "Where the FUCK is the remote?"

By this point, the whole room (except Joey) was crying with laughter. I decided I could only take about three minutes of this impaired friend of mine as he crawled around his hotel room floor looking for the remote. While he unsuccessfully tried to unplug the TV, I put the batteries back in the remote, turned the TV off, and let him know it was me who pranked him.

He started laughing too. And then, pausing in his stupor, he said with a very curious voice, "Wait, you guys ordered a concert on my TV? Like, pay-per-view?"

I said, "Yes, Joey, pay-per-view. And it's an all-day, all-you-can-watch Britney Spears festival."

Somehow, Joey's brain came up with the following realization. "Fucking Fitzpatrick," he said. "What the fuck, man? That's 40 dollars!"

Little did Joey know I'd already left 40 Canadian dollars on his pillow.

Then the perfect rejoinder occurred to me. "Hey Cabral," I said. "You're fully blind, right? Then *how the hell do you know the full Britney package costs 40 Canadian?*"

The room died laughing again, as I explained to Joey that he should check his pillow. He put the money in his wallet. We raised a toast to the game the next day and I left for bed.

I ran Cosain from January 2017 to December 2019.

We won our first contract in April 2017, but I honestly could have worked twice as hard if I wasn't so obsessed with trying to build hockey teams and become a better player. I made a little money on Cosain, but not nearly what I could have made if I'd really applied myself.

I'm a team sport kind of guy, and I found that the lack of social accountability I felt from being a small business founder with only a few employees and a few clients didn't satisfy me or keep me on track. I felt much more fulfilled by hockey.

I realized that if I was going to see a return on the investment I'd made into Cosain, I needed to make more money and cut costs. So I let go of two colleagues, leaving just me and one other employee in the front office, plus our customer-facing teams. I reserved all of my time for one customer for the first time, and assigned myself to the pharmacogenetics lab as their chief information officer. It wasn't the booming growth I dreamed of recreating when I tried to replicate the Akira model of success, but it left me time to pursue my true passions, playing and helping build the game of blind hockey.

Chapter 11

ACHIEVEMENT

Winning the gold medal, having my name inscribed on the Courage Cup, remains to this day the physically hardest thing I've done.

THE YEAR I PUT THE FINISHING TOUCHES on my growth as a hockey player began in a state of conflict with my doctor. I was pressing him, somewhat against his best medical advice, to just slap my leg back together and get me out skating again.

Two factors made this necessary.

First, I'd broken the leg. Or I'd had it broken for me. The incident came about in the most unnecessary fashion, a cheap shot as I've said previously. It was the very end of a game in one of my Saturday night D.C. adult leagues—regulation hockey, not blind hockey, but still a no body-checking situation, as in most adult hockey leagues. With five seconds left in the game, and my team winning by one point, I decided to eat the puck against the wall in one of the corners rather than risk the other team getting a final shot or two on our goalie. This is common practice, totally legal, and very much a good defensive strategy if the situation warrants.

Yet, as the final horn sounded, one of the players on the other team came up hard, charging in to try to dislodge me and the puck. He conducted a maneuver we call "slew-foot," which is illegal, a form of tripping, and a dangerous form at that. Basically, he got his foot behind my foot, his knee behind my knee, so that I went over backward, fulcruming against his leg. Normally the pads in hockey prevent all but the most superficial bruising in situations like this. Unlike other sports where cleats or shoes are meant to grip and stick in the ground, causing all sorts of problems for knees and ankles, the ice in hockey allows things to slip and slide, greatly reducing the chance of most injuries other than those caused by sheer impact.

But I wasn't so lucky.

The toe of my right skate caught in the seam between two sections of boards. My foot stuck as I fell backward, forced by my opponent's illegal slew-foot. My skate stayed in place while the rest of me went down. Something had to give and that something ended up being my fibula.

My doctor fixed it with a titanium plate and seven screws, telling me the injury was thereafter "weight bearing as tolerated." As I left the hospital, even on that first day after the surgery, I said "no thank you" to crutches and walked out under my own power. Later, this injury was part of the genesis for the relationship I mentioned with the orthopedic physician's assistant. But that's a sideline social interaction and not the main focus of this particular year, which really revolved around preparing myself to bring my hockey skills to their most intense level of competitiveness, despite the gruesome injury.

I started skating and training again as soon as I could get my foot into a skate, which was only about two weeks after the surgery. Not a smart thing to do, in terms of healing myself for the long run, but my decisions were driven by the desire to make the Select level of play in Canada, and then, following closely after that, the newly forming Team USA for blind hockey.

All this happened quite quickly.

In 2016, I had played in my first Canadian tournament, seeing the difference between my skill level and the Select level. I spent much of that year playing in every tournament I could find in Canada, and I even hired the Washington Capitals' power skating coach to help me close the gap between the Canadian players and my skating ability. So by the time I saw the orthopedic surgeon in early 2017, I didn't want the injury to hold me back from all the progress I'd made.

The fire that had been lit under me did not diminish when I was accepted to play in the Select Division. I'd been accepted, but I now needed to thrive, not just survive, on the team.

About two weeks after I got that call, making the Selects, was when I took the dirty hit and my leg broke. So all joking aside, I really was skating for a time like I had at least one broken ankle!

I knew I remained a bubble player, having just barely made the Select level. One indication of this was how the teams were divvied up. In blind hockey, victory often goes to the team that ends up with one of the three or four best players. Usually one of them is the hot hand, and the team can ride that player's skill to win the tournament. It's a known thing. If you've got that dominant player on your team, the Jason Yuha or Mark Demontis, you're probably going to win. Usually the organizers try to prevent that from happening, but it often occurs regardless of their best efforts. For the 2017 tourney, the best Canadian player at the time was a guy named Kelly Serbu (Jason Yuha, the Gretzky of blind hockey, hadn't been "found" yet). If you got put on Kelly's team, it meant that the organizers thought you were not as good as the player they matched against you on the other team, as they tried to balance things out. I was put on Kelly's team, I think, for just that reason.

Still, I played hard, got a good amount of ice time in the deciding game of the three-game series. We won the first game. Then I scored my only goal of the tourney in the next game, and it ended up being the game-winner that clinched the gold medal for us.

It went down like this: I took a drop pass from a teammate at the blue line. Then, rather than skating all the way to the net and throwing some kind of razzle-dazzle move on the goalie—mostly because I knew I'd be caught from behind by one of the better skaters on the opposing team if I tried that—I kept the puck on my stick for less than a second. Most blind players don't try this maneuver, which is called "one-timing the puck." It's too hard for us, as we can't see the net when it's far away and we don't do well making quick sight-based adjustments either. But I took an educated guess. The puck seemed to have eyes of its own and the goalie was totally surprised by the shot—being fully blind, he literally didn't see it coming.

There's a funny story about the next few seconds following that goal—and I have video evidence of this. I didn't think I'd score in this tourney, knowing I was back in my role as a try-hard depth player. Therefore, I got pretty darn excited after scoring, and I blacked out for a moment or two. I don't remember it at all. I was windmilling my arms around, high-fiving everyone, with the only problem being that my own teammates had lagged behind the play. The nearest skaters were all from the opposing team. They had been backchecking, trying to catch me. So I was celebrating with the other team, high-fiving them without knowing who they were—a truly blind moment.

I had made big sacrifices during that year, including in my relationship and in my work. I did that consciously, all in the pursuit of getting myself to the point where I could play at the Select level. That goal had risen to be the most important thing in my life. Nothing was going to stop me—not Canadian organizers thinking an American wouldn't be good enough to play at their Select level, nor a broken leg. To this day I have numbness and pain in my ankle, a nasty scar, half of a titanium screw still stuck in my fibula even after the plate was taken out. And my ankle healed so crooked from all of the stress that eventually my right ACL also snapped. That leg just isn't straight or aligned, and it never will be. Even with all those things, I ended up with every member of that Canadian team signing a jersey for me at the awards ceremony, and I keep it framed on my wall. Every time I need some motivation I look at it.

There are times where work, or a relationship, can get physically difficult. Other times in my life, like at the Air Force Academy or playing sports when I was younger, also presented significant physical challenges. Yet being on that Canadian team, winning the gold medal, having my name inscribed on the Courage Cup, remains to this day the physically hardest thing I've done. Having achieved such a milestone, and having the jersey and medal to reflect on, makes the rest of my life feel easier when I need some perspective.

In the beginning of 2018, after the Courage Cup, I started to catch wind of the possibility that USA Hockey might sanction a blind hockey team.

I was invited to try out for it. But I hadn't fully recovered from the ankle surgery. I was in the midst of my third round of physical therapy as I tried to get my foot, ankle, and tendons back in alignment. I went to see a doctor in Denver recommended by some friends at the pharmacogenetic clinic where I was working as their CIO-for-hire. He offered me some treatments to help complete my recovery.

In February 2018, having confirmed the rumors that there would be a blind hockey national team selection tournament in Chicago later that spring, I began undergoing these therapies. The treatments lasted about four months, and they worked—I got all my strength back in my right leg, and I was ready to compete for the ultimate blind hockey honor of playing for my country. I was 41 years old, outskating 25-year-olds on the ice while I trained at Denver University.

To be honest, even though I certainly was excited to get the calls—both the one inviting me to compete in the tryout and the follow-up call that I'd made the team—I never doubted that this would be the outcome. I knew I wasn't the best player in America, but I felt certain I ranked as one of the best five or six. All my efforts getting my game up to Canadian standards made that a virtual certainty. What most excited me about the possibility, though, was how many of the players I'd helped get into blind hockey would now also get the chance to participate. I'd had a hand in initiating the hockey journeys for at least half of those who had been invited to try out. And now I would get to skate alongside them on our national team!

I decided to put the finishing touches on my preparation for the camp in a somewhat unique way. I'd been training in the most progressive fashion, at altitude in Denver, with a personal trainer, high-intensity interval sessions specifically designed for a blind guy—box jumps and ladder runs and similar stuff that we customized for a low-vision participant. We installed bright-pink sticky notes on the edges of boxes for box jumps and fluorescent-green hockey tape to the edges of all the objects he had me pick up and move, or sprint between, helping me navigate almost all the same types of training an NFL player would go through in preparation for the combine. But, beyond that, I'd also stumbled on something really outside the scope of a modern workout regimen. One of the other guys from the tryout in Chicago was a legally blind lobsterman from Maine named Dirk Morgan. Dirk was the kind of player I wanted to play like—a lunch-pail, hard-nosed, physical forward, about 50 pounds heavier than me, who had grown up scrapping his way through youth hockey on the central coast of Maine. I loved his game and suspected he might be my linemate on Team USA. Dirk mentioned in passing during a break in the tryout's intense drills and scrimmages that he conducted most of his workouts on the deck of a lobster boat.

I said, "Holy shit, I've got to see this."

I planned my whole vacation that summer around getting out there to Maine, telling him I would only come if he agreed to let me work the boat for a day. And that he did.

I woke up that morning at 3:45 AM, needing to be at his house by 4:30. It was August at this time, so not too cold. Yet in Maine the water never warms too much; otherwise, it wouldn't hold a good population of lobsters. (That being said: global warming and the couple degree temperature rise in Maine's waters have in the last decade really put a damper on professional lobstering, with most of the lobster we eat in the U.S. now coming from further north in Nova Scotia.)

That August day dawned as mild and pleasant as you can expect on the water in Maine. The Morgan family had done well for themselves in the lobstering business. They owned their own boat, which is the dream for a lot of people in Maine. And with the proceeds from their business they had built a nice single-family home, complete with a horse jumping stable out back.

I hopped in the back of their truck on the way to the boat. Dirk's father—who I've only ever called Captain Morgan since first laying eyes on him—turned around and with wicked New Englander humor, told me, "You're going to be the bait bitch."

I asked what a bait bitch was, and he said, "Well, you're going to need a long shower at the end of the day."

When we arrived at the marina, Captain Morgan purchased a 55-gallon drum of dead fish called porgies. He opened the lid and explained to me that my job would be to spend the day stabbing them so that their rotten scent would attract lobsters to the traps. I nearly fainted from the noxious greasy fumes.

A small lobstering boat usually operates with three personnel. The captain drives. The first mate pulls the traps up and inspects the lobsters to make sure they are regulation-sized—if they're too large or too small they have to be thrown back. The third guy baits the traps and prepares them to go back in the water. Having a fourth person in the boat is a luxury. Usually the baiter, being the low man on the totem pole, runs a great risk because he has to turn around and step over the trap line. That line can drag you to the bottom if your foot gets caught in it.

Since I was there, adding a fourth person to the operation, they let me stand a relatively safe distance away from Dirk, maybe eight feet behind him, on the other side from that death line, prepping porgies between the rounds of pulling traps. We spent eight, almost nine hours on the water that day, from 5:00 AM to until about 3:00 PM, getting back to the marina around 4:00. While the boat navigated between islands, searching out the buoys painted with the Morgan family's unique color pattern (each family or lobstering operation has its own colors to help distinguish whose line is whose), the baiting and hauling of traps would cease for a bit. During those intervals, Dirk took me to the back of the boat and together we did boat yoga—which proved especially challenging. Balancing on a moving, swaying boat isn't the easiest even for fully sighted people. For blind guys like us, we were even more challenged! (Try it for yourself: close your eyes and stand on one foot, even on a solid, non-swaying floor. It's tough!)

I kept my yoga moves as basic as possible, while Dirk did all the fancy stuff: single-leg lunges, all those crazy additions to the poses where a yogi wraps their leg around their neck like a scarf. Having just finished my third round of rehab on my leg, I found the experience to be a good test of balance before training camp. I'd done everything that science could do for me, so this helped level me up. I was not against a bit of woo-woo yoga magic and lobster boat toughness, if those things could make me even 1 percent better.

Dirk and I hit the ice a couple times during that week in Portland too. And I was able to pay back some of his kindness in hosting me and teaching me to lobster by helping him make better connections at the Portland ice rink. Being a very extroverted guy and having spent so much time over the past few years liaising with various NHL and blind hockey organizations, such conversations came second nature to me. I simply called up the local rink, explained that Dirk and I were going to go do this really hard thing, playing for the USA blind hockey team, and the manager of the rink—who was a prime example of a Mainer—immediately donated ice time for us so we could get out there with our rattling steel-shelled blind-hockey pucks.

Lobstering is a very superstitious pastime, just as any fishing tends to be. At the beginning of that first day, in addition to making me the bait bitch, Captain Morgan told me that, for my own sake, I had better not be a "Jonah." The origin of that was Jonah and the whale from the Bible, and I was vaguely aware that it had become nautical slang for someone who is a curse. Captain Morgan was informing me, in no uncertain terms, that I had better not bring bad luck to the boat. Yet they ended up with their best catch of the year. Once the tank filled with 500 pounds of prime Maine lobsters, Dirk and I had to start filling Home Depot five-gallon buckets with saltwater to catch the overflow, a great problem to have on a lobster boat. As we pulled into the marina at the day's end, Captain Morgan said, "Well, Fitzy, I guess you're not a Jonah," and he told Dirk to give me some lobsters.

I'd spent the whole of the preceding week eating lobster. Too much of it. After the first few days, I did not want more. I'd had enough. So I demurred, but Dirk's father insisted. And I ended up with six choice lobsters plucked fresh from the tank and tossed in a bucket. I looked at Dirk with an expression meant to say: *What the hell am I supposed to do with these?*

After taking a 45-minute shower that night to get the fish smell off me, I came down to their dining room to find a silver tray with corn and potatoes, and all six of those lobsters cooked and ready to eat.

I asked Dirk, "Are you joining me?"

He laughed. "We don't eat lobster."

I managed to consume about one and a half of the little beasts, then together we picked the tail and claw meat free from the remaining shells, bagged it, and brought it with us as a gift to both the coach and general manager of Team USA the next day when we showed up to training camp, both of us still probably smelling vaguely of seawater and unctuous porgies.

The training camp for Team USA lasted four days and was held in August 2018 at Utica College in upstate New York. The roster for the team had been announced at a banquet on the last night of the selection tournament in Chicago in May, and the president of USA Hockey, Jim Smith, delivered the news to all of us who had spent our time and energy trying to make the team. It was a cool moment. Twenty-three players received invitations to the camp, although there had been no predefined roster size. This was, after all, the first U.S. Blind Hockey Team, and I think the coaching staff's main motivation was to field as many players as possible who would not embarrass themselves against Canada.

The head coach, a guy named Mike Svac, formed part of what I like to call the "Chicago Mafia" of USA disabled hockey—a group that revolved around Jim Smith. A lot of the blind hockey community knows that I had a falling out with Mike. I will always respect Mike for the time he's given to blind hockey. He is neither blind nor does he have a blind kid himself—so he's really done all this altruistically, helping those who are less fortunate even without a direct connection to blindness. He helped found the Chicago Blackhawks Blind

Hockey Club, which is a first-rate organization, and he's done a ton to support blind hockey in many other ways, both on the ice and off.

That said, Mike—and all of the other coaches for that first national team—had very limited experience communicating with, guiding, or coaching blind athletes. The first training camp, like many entrepreneurial ventures, turned into a bit of a mess. But being an entrepreneur myself, I embraced the mess.

At the time, USA Hockey as an overarching entity—including regulation hockey and all the disabled programs—had committed itself to what it called the American Development Model, which centers around a series of drills designed to help players compete in small spaces. The idea is to stickhandle with lots of challenges, make quick decisions, and keep a fast tempo. Mike, as a Level Five USA Hockey coach, was a disciple of this model.

The problem however, at least for blind people, is that most of us at this early stage still needed to learn to orient ourselves on the ice. We needed to practice together the major movements of hockey: learning how to figure out where the goal is, where the bench is, where that pesky blue line for offside would be. We needed to smooth out our navigation and teach ourselves the proprioception of skating via means other than eyesight. The coaches, in forcing us to train primarily via this American Development Model, took all opportunity of that away. Instead they favored moving nets into the corners or other alternate locations; having us run cross-ice drills; and just generally limiting our ability to learn to navigate the ice as a cohesive unit.

Even with that flawed coaching paradigm, we did begin, ever so slowly, to jell. As we came together, we played several exhibition games against sighted teams, a cool experience and one the opposition sides seemed to enjoy. One such friendly game pitted us against players from the AHL Utica Comets (the AHL being the primary professional development league for the NHL, akin to baseball's minor leagues or to Division I college football as a recruiting ground for the NFL). This game ended up being hilariously lopsided. The AHL skaters were way out of our league, and they had to really hold back, but they seemed to appreciate the experience, and we drew a great crowd.

We also had a series of unique, kind of surreal experiences. We had our photos taken just like other Team USA members. We received media training. We bonded over lots of team meals as we wore our USA gear. It was the real thing, and I felt immensely proud to be part of it.

Now, of course, I was still me—a little too adventuresome and always willing to push the envelope.

One night, one of my camp roommates, Mark DeFlorio, and I snuck out. I know the statute of limitations for being kicked off Team USA by Mike Svac has passed for me; I no longer play. And I'll assume the same for Mark, who is still involved with the program. I was 41 at the time, Mark in his late thirties, and we'd been paired together. There was a strict no booze policy at camp, which I found ridiculous for grown adults. So I called an Uber to the campus dorm we bunked in, and I had the driver, who I found out was named Scott Walker, take us to a Chinese restaurant downtown. On the way to dinner, we explained why we were in town, and the driver actually knew about the camp—advertisements for the exhibition game with the AHL team had been on the radio. He mentioned that he had a six-year-old son, Axel, who happened to be visually impaired and was also trying to play hockey. I couldn't believe the coincidence. As the only Uber driver in town that night—Utica is tiny—he ended up as our driver again later and took us from dinner to a bar. I asked if he'd just go off the clock, wait for us for a bit, and take us home from there. I paid him cash and we got to talking about how his son had been bullied for wearing huge, thick glasses, and what a big hockey fan he had somehow become. I had probably five beers in me by this point, so I didn't consider the repercussions of my next move: inviting Scott and his son to the following day's game. Axel came to our practice that next morning before the game, and I ambushed Mike with the details right before we got on the ice—making it so that our hard-ass coach had no real choice but to say yes to any involvement I dreamed up for the kid. Axel had brought his gear, as I requested, and I ushered him out onto the ice for the last few minutes of our practice the morning before the game. Axel went head-to-head against my dear friend Doug Goist, by that point the goalie for Team USA and—if you remember—one of the first guys I'd convinced to try blind hockey. Doug reprised his earlier move from our first Try Blind Hockey session by letting Axel score a goal on him. Axel was thrilled. His parents cheered next to the glass. And our whole team got pretty pumped up to see how excited Axel was.

It was a good reminder that this was exactly why I was still playing hockey.

Axel's whole family came to the game that night against the Utica Comets. We took a bunch of photos afterward. And our families have been in touch since. Axel's parents brought him down to Pittsburgh for the USA vs. Canada game later on, and I gave him a piggyback ride around the rink afterward in my USA jersey.

Giving Axel a piggyback around the rink after he and his family joined us in Pittsburgh, where I represented the USA against Canada in the first-ever international blind hockey series in 2018.

Chapter 12

TEAM USA

Putting on No. 9 for Team USA created a renewed sense of urgency for me to be of service to the blind community. That sense of urgency far outweighed the honor of playing for the team itself.

PLAYING ON TEAM USA for blind hockey had two distinct phases, both of which opened my eyes in significant ways. The first of these phases—actually playing an international competition against Team Canada—I knew would be tough. The second phase—dealing with conflict between my place on Team USA and my place in helping other blind people participate in the sport—caught me by surprise and made me reassess what was really important to me about sport and about life in general.

Wearing America's uniform has meant a great deal to me since I was a kid. It formed part of my calling to serve when I decided I wanted to go to the Air Force Academy. I planned to wear a military uniform for an entire career thereafter in the Air Force. For this reason, putting a uniform back on that represented my country, when I made Team USA, came with a whole flood of emotions. The most important emotion it brought to mind was the obligation to serve others, especially blind people in need. One of the core values of the Air Force is "service before self." Putting on No. 9 for Team USA created a renewed sense of urgency for me to be of service to the blind community. That sense of urgency far outweighed the honor of playing for the team itself.

We "won" a silver medal in that first international blind hockey tournament. But to call it a win is a bit of a mirage, really, as there were only two teams: us and the Canadians. If the previous few chapters about the advantages of Canadian hockey culture over its American stepchild haven't already made this clear, the games weren't even close. We'd signed up for two three-game tournaments, one in the U.S. and a follow-up later in the year in Canada, yet the tourney in Pittsburgh showed the Canadian organizers how far behind we really were.

The scores were:

Game 1: Canada 8, USA 2
Game 2: Canada 12, USA 3
Game 3: Canada 6, USA 2

Team Canada threw their gloves off and mobbed their goalie when they won the second game, securing their gold medals, and I was glad for them. I knew most of those guys, knew how hard they'd worked, and I took my sweet time in the handshake line congratulating my friends.

While the outcome looked lopsided in the extreme, the event itself represented a first significant step toward blind hockey becoming a Paralympic sport. Americans and Canadians had been playing in blind hockey tournaments together for four years at this point, though scrambled onto teams. This was the first time two countries played each other. USA Hockey officially sanctioned blind hockey as a disabled discipline of hockey in 2017, which meant that it had recognized the rules we'd developed for the sport. Officials were tasked to learn those rules. And blind hockey started to be played annually at the USA Hockey Disabled Festival. That event mainly highlights sled hockey, because so many more people play it, especially kids. Yet even being included in the festival gave our version of the game legitimacy and provided a point of entry to the sport for a significant number of blind players who otherwise would never have heard of the sport, and therefore never would have gotten to compete.

The lead-up to that first tournament in Pittsburgh had been eventful for the whole team.

As mentioned, the first step was the selection event in Chicago in the spring of 2018. I continued to train in Denver through the summer, but then went to Maine to spend that time with Dirk Morgan just ahead of the training camp in Utica, New York, in August. USA Hockey officially announced the roster for the team in September 2018. Since the selected players lived all over the U.S. and the team had no budget to support player travel, we never practiced together as a group before we arrived in Pittsburgh that October. We went right from drills at an individual level—that concept of the American Development Model, which features quick reactions in limited space—to playing the Canadians on a full sheet of ice, never having worked together as lines, never having devoted time to practice the more fluid and team-oriented aspects of the game.

The first time I actually put the USA jersey on was when they called my name as part of the team in Chicago in May 2018. We held an initial exhibition game in August during the training camp in Utica, wearing the same jerseys. So by the time we got to Pittsburgh and were doing it for real, I'd played in the same piece of fabric six times. USA Hockey wouldn't pay for jerseys for the players to keep, so the team was only able to get one set of jerseys with no names on them, intending them to be used year after year, at least until more fundraising could happen. To his credit, the coach, Mike

Svac, took on a great deal of that fundraising to get the team what we needed for this tournament, though the budget never allowed for individual jerseys with our names and numbers.

I asked to play in No. 98, my college graduation year. It being Team USA, I wanted to give a nod to my Air Force Academy classmates and the military sacrifices they'd made. But since we only got one set of jerseys, we didn't get to pick our numbers; the jerseys purchased for the team only went up to number 30 or so. I took No. 9 as a consolation—the closest I could get to 98. Over the coming months I grew to really like the number, so that now it seems a natural fit for me.

During the preceding few years when I had been flying to any blind hockey tournament I could get to, I played with most of the players on Team Canada, and I knew we were going to have a rough ride. A couple of my teammates also anticipated the situation. Team Canada boasted multiple players who'd risen all the way through Junior-level hockey—basically the Canadian equivalent of Division I competition—before losing their vision. We on Team USA had no one with comparable experience. We had selected two women to the team—something of which I'm incredibly proud, not because they were women but because they were legitimately the best available players. We also named a fully blind skater to the team—something Canada didn't do. The deck was definitely stacked against us. But our coaches, coming from disabled hockey more generally rather than from the more specific world of blind hockey, had no clue what we were up against. A few of us mentioned that we would be best off playing an essentially defensive game, picking our spots to counterattack. But our coaching staff was confident—so confident, in fact, that we spent half of our morning skate before Game 1 practicing penalty shots in case the game went to a shootout.

Many of us found this hilarious. We didn't review break-out schemes, because we had none. We didn't review our lines, who we were paired up with, because they hadn't been set. We did penalty shots—hubris in the extreme, given the state of our team and who we were facing.

A typical blind hockey tournament unfolds with one game Friday, one Saturday, and one Sunday. This first international tournament in Pittsburgh was no different. A sly hope of mine in these situations was always to have the tournament decided by Saturday—my team winning or losing both of the first two games—so I could go enjoy whatever city I was visiting. For this Pittsburgh match, I was so convinced we'd lose that I had already booked dinner reservations for Saturday night for my mom in downtown Pittsburgh.

I don't remember much of the lead-up before the actual first game because I was so busy taking care of everyone else. A blind hockey locker room is a real-life example of "in the land of the blind, the one-eyed man is king." I could see better than six or seven of my teammates, so I often helped find pieces of equipment that had dropped behind the bench or handed out 5-Hour Energy drinks (my pregame ritual having, by this time, shifted from beer to Red Bull) or inserted myself as the locker room DJ. This caretaking behavior also connected me strongly to my teen years, when I'd assumed that role with my siblings after my father's death. It was a natural fit and formed the bedrock of who I was as a player and teammate—that try-hard guy who was going to do everything possible to help others, even at the expense of soaking up the memories of that historic moment before we first stepped on the ice to compete as Team USA.

I do remember being the last one out of the locker room, though. There, in the doorway, as I readied myself to stride across the rubberized mats and onto the crisp white sheet of coldness within the clanging boards, our team general manager and guardian angel, Doris Donley, waited with the keys to lock the locker room door.

I winked at Doris and said, "This ought to be...interesting."

She slapped me on the shoulder pads, like any great hockey mom would likely do, and she told me to have a great game.

Those were a punishing three days. Team USA only fielded 14 skaters, and two of them couldn't finish, which left us with just two lines and one extra substitute—a huge load in terms of skating time, especially when the opposing team is skating circles around you. In Game 2, that Saturday, I blocked a shot from Jason Yuha, the best blind hockey player on either of the teams. It struck my left foot and dropped me. Made of 22-gauge steel, the blind puck is heavier and harder than a vulcanized rubber regulation puck—very painful when it hits you. My foot swelled before Game 3, but I forced my skate on, knowing I had to play since two of my teammates couldn't. I found out after I got back to D.C. that I broke a tarsal bone on my left foot, adding to my accumulating litany of lower body injuries.

Following our silver medal effort in Pittsburgh, I went on to play in the Western Canada Blind Hockey Championship in November 2018. I'd participated in this tournament in each of the previous three years, with U.S. and Canadian players scrambling onto teams at the beginning of the event.

Then, in March 2019, because Team Canada had absolutely pounded Team USA in Pittsburgh, the organizers decided to split the Canadian team into Team East and Team West to play against Team USA in the Select Division. Team USA fared a little better with this new format, even pulling ahead in the first game of the competition with a couple of timely goals.

One of the best and most lasting moments of all this time happened back in the Pittsburgh tournament. My mom had been in the stands. She had seen me wearing that Team USA jersey and came down to give me a big hug and tell me how proud she was of me. Following that moment, Axel—the kid I had met through his father's Uber driving in Utica—came running down to the locker room, gave me a big hug, and told me he was proud of me as well. Again I picked him up and told him I was proud of him too for starting to play hockey, for not letting his eyesight stop him from pursuing things he liked and wanted to do in life. I carried him around the rink in my USA jersey, outside the glass, with my skates on. That moment crystallized for me, making me realize that I had accomplished something by going on the ice and enduring a painful series of defeats. Along with my teammates, coaches, and volunteers, I'd provided inspiration for future players, young blind kids who were probably afraid of what life held in store for them. I realized that this, helping others rather than competing myself, really formed the underpinning of my devotion to the sport.

As a result, between that tournament in Pittsburgh in October 2018 and the following tournament in Canada in March 2019, I renewed my motivation to reach out to NHL teams in my effort to build the charity that USA Hockey had asked me to start—a new 501(c)(3) called the U.S. Blind Hockey Association. This would be my second 501(c)(3). I still operated, although on a more limited scale, my original Washington Wheelers charity, and I'd helped other programs start their own local 501(c)(3) organizations. This one was nationwide, with the express mission to coordinate fundraising for other clubs around the country that didn't have their own non-profit systems, removing the tax barrier and making any contributions deductible, and thereby hopefully kickstarting a number of other programs.

Unfortunately, even though USA Hockey's Disabled Division Leader, JJ O'Connor, advised me to start this charity—similar but more focused on blind hockey than their pre-existing U.S. Special Hockey Association non-profit—JJ decided to reverse course in January 2019. Not only did he direct that we shut down the new 501(c)(3), but he also told me to stop organizing Try Blind Hockey events altogether.

I told him no.

By this point I had made significant progress with the Carolina Hurricanes, Philadelphia Flyers, Las Vegas Golden Knights, and Arizona Coyotes, professional teams that wanted to promote the game. I'd also sunk roughly seven thousand more dollars of my own money in the effort because of the difficulties that Bobby, the conniving director of the BVA grant program, had caused getting our funding shut down.

USA Hockey's Disabled Section had apparently discovered some problems with the fundraising efforts of the U.S. Special Hockey Association. They wanted to reel everything back under the umbrella of USA Hockey more generally. The real problem with this was that, apparently for liability reasons, they mandated that a regional representative from their organization would thereafter be required to attend and supervise every Try Blind Hockey event. Yet their representatives had neither experience with blind hockey nor a robust enough footprint to support the upwelling interest I'd started to create with all these NHL teams. For example, they had one representative for the whole Southeast Region of the U.S., and trying to get him, as a classic bureaucrat, to drive personally from where he lived in Alabama to cover Nashville, Raleigh, and Tampa was just impossible. It was neither fair to him nor to the kids who were excited to try blind hockey for the first time; they'd be held back because of bureaucracy. At this point in the growth of blind hockey, just like in business, I had learned that momentum was everything and slowing down was death.

I wasn't interested in slowing down. I knew I had opened a window in my life where I had time I wouldn't always have, time in which I could make as much impact for as many kids' lives as possible. I genuinely believed that it couldn't be wrong to do what in my heart I knew was best for blind kids like Axel. Whether I wore the Team USA jersey or not, this would be my calling.

Leading up to the second tournament against Team Canada, which would be hosted in Toronto, this conflict came to a head.

USA Disabled Hockey is organized into various disciplines. A man named Kevin Shanley led the discipline of blind hockey. Kevin had, like me, also been selected to play on Team USA, although as a defenseman. So he was both my teammate and my collaborator in trying to grow blind hockey for a period of time. He and I cofounded the U.S. Blind Hockey Association non-profit. He also, unfortunately, ended up being the person through whom the orders came to shut it down. It put us in the awkward position of being teammates and one-time collaborators who got recast as competitors. Kevin bought into the demands from USA Disabled Hockey to shut down the non-profit. When I disagreed with him, he sent a nationwide email in January 2019 announcing that I was trying to start an organization competing with USA Blind Hockey and organize separate blind hockey teams.

That was untrue.

All I wanted to do was try to get as many blind people on the ice as possible, growing the sport any way I could. I simply decided I was going to keep organizing Try Blind Hockey events with or without the support of USA Hockey. So I went through with the events I had planned with the Philadelphia Flyers and the Carolina Hurricanes in February 2019. I basically gave USA Hockey the middle finger by proceeding with those events. They were successful too—putting more than 65 blind children onto the ice and getting donations worth over $50,000 in equipment from Leveling the Playing Field, the same organization that had come through in a pinch to support my first Try Blind Hockey event in D.C. The equipment went directly to the North Carolina and Overbrook (Philadelphia) Schools for the Blind, so neither of the 501(c)(3)s touched the funds.

At this point, the conflict boiled over onto Team USA. Mike Svac sent another email three weeks before the tournament. Although worded just vaguely enough to give him a fig leaf, its content clearly targeted me. He wrote, "I want to remind all of you again that you are representing Team USA from the time you arrive until the time you depart.... I do not want any distractions while we are in Canada.... Option 1—You represent Team USA or Option 2—You can participate in the tournament with other players from USA and Canada."

The Open Division was basically a demotion. Remember, the Select Division, in Canadian parlance, represented the topmost level of play, and its winners' names were inscribed on the Courage Cup.

I read the email and took it as both directed at me (which I'm sure it was) and bad for the team, bad for blind hockey. To Mike, at that time, the email was about control, not what was best for the sport or for the team, certainly not what was best for the kids I was trying to help. Mike is an upper Midwestern hard-ass who worked in manufacturing for most of his career, in compliance or regulatory affairs, I believe. As a result, he tended to see things in black and white. While I'll always be grateful for him giving his time to coach and while I genuinely believe he raised his hand to coach the team because he wanted to help, I didn't feel the stance he took was something I could abide.

I felt betrayed. The coach of Team USA had put me on blast. Everyone knew the email was about me, or at least knew about the conflict between my efforts and the position USA Hockey had taken with regard to its liabilities during Try Blind Hockey events. Coach Svac said, with only the faintest attempt at veiling his position, that the conflict I caused had better not be a distraction in Toronto.

I decided I wasn't going to back down or stop organizing blind hockey events for people who wanted access to the sport. I took the moment to make a choice. *What is more important to me: Putting on No. 9 for Team USA again or putting 90 more blind athletes onto the ice this year?*

The answer came easily. I didn't hesitate. I called our sweetheart of a general manager, the same Doris Donley who I continue to think of as the guardian angel of blind hockey. She has an amazing heart and always gives great advice. I explained my thoughts to her, and she told me she was so sorry I found myself in this situation and that I should trust my heart and make the choice I thought was best. (Doris, by the way, would go on to take over as the USA Blind Hockey rep after Kevin Shanley left later that year. She and I have remained close.)

I got off the phone with her, slept on the situation, and the next day sent Mike Svac an email accepting his proposition and telling him that I thought it would indeed be best that for the 2019 Canadian Blind Hockey Championship in Toronto, I play in the Open Division and not be a distraction to the team. I did not tell him I was resigning from Team USA, but that I thought it would be better to play in a different division for that tournament. Basically, I sent myself to the minor leagues for that one weekend, or so I thought.

By this time, I already knew that Mike didn't like me and frankly, the feeling was kind of mutual. Along with a few other players, I had been critical of his adherence to the American Development Model of teaching hockey, especially at the expense of figuring out what specific needs blind hockey players would have in learning a higher level of the game. Mike took my email as his opportunity to remove me from the team permanently. He immediately sent an announcement to the team saying that I had resigned from Team USA and that an alternate would fill my spot going forward.

Now, on the surface, that might seem like a shitty way to go out.

No one likes to leave a team or a situation on a note like that.

But, at the same time, my attitude was a bit different. Every one of those blind hockey tournaments had been special to me, because I never knew if I'd get another one. I might get hurt. I might have something happen at work that required me to drop the game. As a result, I really focused on enjoying the 2019 Canadian Blind Hockey Championship, even as I competed at the lower Open level. The locker room climate was more fun. The striving and the futile attempt to compete with the Canadians disappeared. A few of my teammates and I went across the street from the ice rink to an Irish bar near Maple Leaf Gardens after one of the games. There we saw six of my former Team USA teammates walk in. I couldn't recognize them as individuals from across the room, but they wore the team warm-up uniforms, and I could clearly see their hunched backs and dejected attitudes after once again being beaten—this time by only half of the Canadian roster. I sent one of them a beer. And he came over to tell me, as part of Mike's new rules, he wasn't allowed to drink it.

This drove home the point for me—I showed up to events like this for such different reasons from so many other people who just wanted to take something from blind hockey; experience, notoriety, a moment of fame. Sure, those things are nice. But the comradery for me rose to such a level—and so much of it involves getting a beer, letting our guard down—that the idea of prohibiting grown men and women, who were not playing these games for money or any kind of advantage, from having a beer after the game struck me as really shortsighted, a viewpoint that missed what was most important.

Sitting down with other blind people, blind athletes, after a game, having a beer, talking about the rest of our lives that often have nothing to do with hockey, that is an experience great for my soul. I would often find myself in those moments giving career advice to a twentysomething guy who had recently lost his eyesight. Perhaps he was scared shitless, not knowing if he'd find a job, get married, be able to go on a date, or figure out where he was going to live. That was what I showed up for at these tournaments and events. That, and the chance to help kids embrace the sport for many of the same reasons: to open their horizons, make them realize their lives would still be filled with possibility, despite their blindness.

Competing in the Open Division rather than on Team USA was in fact a perfect—not shitty—way to go out.

I got to do the two things that meant the most to me about blind hockey: pay it forward to other adults, especially since I felt a little guilty to have attained the life situation I'd managed to reach (having a college degree and four years of work experience before being diagnosed with Stargardt disease, which I knew was just the luck of the draw) and getting to see a little of myself every time I sat down with a blind athlete to talk about life. Sometimes those conversations are easier to have over a beer or two. If a coach didn't understand that or didn't want to listen to it, if Mike wanted to be a hard-ass and didn't trust a fortysomething-year-old man to make good decisions, then I wanted nothing to do with him.

Just like this tough choice with Team USA, I've had to make a lot of hard choices in my career. Deciding what is most important to me in my work has been easier because of the perspective I gained making that hard decision with Team USA. At one level, in the moments after receiving the email from Mike Svac and consulting with Doris Donley, I reached down into my gut emotions, into how I really felt about the situation. What upwelled from that I really learned to appreciate: a prioritization based not on ego or artificial and exterior recognition, but the true rationale behind my passion for organizing and playing blind hockey.

I've similarly made a number of important business decisions based on my gut rather than objective individual measures of success. The process of being nudged off Team USA worked out okay for me and gave me confidence to trust that sort of decision. One example of this: I took a flier on putting my intellectual happiness at work ahead of money the following year, leaving a very high-powered and potentially high-paying job in Baton Rouge and coming back to D.C. to work with a start-up in AI and quantum technologies. That story I'll save for the next chapter or two, but now, looking back on how Team USA shaped me, I realize I followed the same playbook—going with my gut and choosing the happiness of mind and heart ahead of other things. Objective success, as measured in Team USA or the title of COO, would come third on my list of priorities.

Chapter 13

SOUL

What you accomplish in life can only live on through others.
Teaching others to play blind hockey lit that light bulb for me.
And it changed who I am as a person.

THE LESSON I LEARNED through all this—through the uncertainty, the suffering, the hard work, the successes, and the joy—has been that real goodness doesn't come from trophies or paychecks. It manifests in the impact we have on others. That's what makes my soul happy, to see the impact of my effort improving other people's lives.

Over a period of three years, I spent countless hours of my time, massive chunks of my energy and emotional bandwidth, and more than $50,000 of my own money participating in and pushing for the formation of blind hockey in the United States. I formed the Washington Wheelers club from nothing. I helped start the U.S. Blind Hockey Association. I doubled down on my efforts to put kids on the ice by propagating the model of the Wheelers across other major cities with NHL clubs in the United States. All this external effort wrought changes in me internally too. For example, when working out, my visualization of success shifted from that of raising my hands after scoring a goal to that of tying a kid's skates, helping another blind child take those first important steps toward building confidence by participating in team sports. I was using the individual hockey success I'd found as a platform to fill in the hole in my soul that not having kids of my own left. I also started to envision myself in terms of longevity, of being healthy and fit enough over the coming years to hopefully tie my own kids' skates someday.

This represented a change in how I measured my success as a man, a very different perspective than I had taken over my first 40 years on this planet. I didn't have children of my own, and the D.C. Try Blind Hockey event had helped me experience the joy of seeing other blind people—especially children—experience the exhilarating freedom of being on the ice for the first time. So I started counting, how many blind people had I helped and how many could I help get access to ice skating and hockey? There were 73 of us at the first event in D.C. Then 38 more new athletes who joined the program in D.C. over the course of the year in 2017. Likewise, our 2016 event in Colorado Springs brought 22 new blind athletes—again mostly children—into the sport. And that's where I first came into contact with Doris Donley to boot. The guardian angel of blind hockey was at that time in charge of disabled hockey in Colorado. So going there, bringing the goodness of the model of the Wheelers to Colorado, ended up bringing great people like Doris into my life as an added benefit.

All told, I planned, managed, and participated in 14 Try Blind Hockey events in D.C., Pittsburgh, Denver, San Jose, Nashville (just ball hockey in a gym, but still), Raleigh, St. Louis, and Philadelphia. At my last count, the sum total of blind people who experienced ice skating or hockey for the first time through these events amounted to 310 individuals. When I die, I believe that helping this number of disabled people will be one of my proudest and most significant accomplishments.

Introducing visually impaired kids to the sport I love at Try Blind Hockey events has been one of the most rewarding experiences of my life.

I found joy in working with both kids and adults. But since I've always been a big kid at heart—probably because I didn't get much of a childhood myself—I took the most joy in working with blind children. Three things really touched me in working with them:

1. Their parents' reactions. I think every parent focuses instinctually on protecting their children, and that probably ends up being an even more intense protective instinct if the child has a disability. I imagine if my kid were blind, I'd have some baseline level of fear every time they left the house to do anything. As a result, my protectiveness might actually harm the child by holding them back from life, from growth, from experiences. My favorite moment with a lot of the kids,

which would happen at different times, different stages on the ice, involved seeing the light bulb go on for the parent, that moment when they'd realize, *My kid can do this.*

2. The kids' resilience. I've seen so many kids grow up as spoiled little brats, electronic devices always in their hands, whining and back-talking to their parents, expecting their every wish to be fulfilled. Blind kids aren't like that. They've been humbled and they've learned how to get back up every time life kicks the shit out of them and knocks them down. Blind kids also infrequently complain. They have a deep-seated determination that makes them want to stay on skates long after their legs are tired from wobbling around the first time they hit the ice. I've coached both sighted and blind kids and adults on the ice. We'd always have some volunteers who weren't great at skating themselves but really wanted to help blind people. Siblings to blind kids would also want to try skating—and that was a great thing because I knew that if you involved a parent or sibling with their blind family member on the ice they would be that much more likely to stick with it. No disparagement to fully sighted kids, but blind kids I think are often tougher. They pop up quicker when they fall. They've got more at stake, more they need to prove to the world, to their parents, to their siblings.
3. Their gratitude. I don't mean that being thanked is some kind of ego boost. I'm not particularly interested in personal thanks. But I find it amazing to see how thankful blind kids are to be there in the first place, getting to do something that even some fully sighted kids might be too afraid to try. Kids seem so happy when pushing their boundaries, growing their abilities and broadening their experiences. Also: good luck trying to get 20 blind kids off the ice at the end of a session—they don't want to leave in the first place, and then it takes them forever to find the door!

My joy and pride working with blind kids also ties back strongly to my own childhood. Not just losing my dad, but also becoming the stand-in father for my siblings—especially for Brendan, who suffered from and overcame so many disabilities—means that I have a real deep-seated place in my soul for supporting others. The feeling I get when I spend time on the ice helping a blind child become a blind athlete and a blind hockey player specifically is similar to the feeling I got when I helped raise Brendan (although now not so tangled up in my own teen angst and suffering, trying to figure out who I was and how to function in the world without a father).

I've always wanted kids of my own.

I'm an irrationally optimistic person—borderline delusional—when it comes to life goals, so a part of me always believed I would have a family of my own. But, to be honest, I think I acted out a lot of hopes I'd had for a family through the blind kids I worked with. For example, I met these two albino blind children in D.C.—Nate and Aiden McCown—early on when we were building the D.C. team. Their dad, Mike, didn't know how to skate very well, but he'd enrolled himself in the same hockey school I attended. As a result, we became friends. I actually went back to novice-level regulation hockey while playing on Team USA in order to skate for a season as Mike's defense partner.

At this time, back in 2017, I was still a pretty heavy drinker. We were just starting to expand our program with the Wheelers and our ice time at the Caps' rink remained anchored to that lovely Sunday morning 6:00 AM slot. Mike told me once that he had to make Nate and Aiden go back to bed early on Sundays because they'd regularly wake up before 4:00 AM and start putting their gear on. That's how excited they were to get to the rink! Many a morning I only succeeded in fighting off a hangover, calling a $35 Uber to get from my house to the rink (30 minutes away), by gritting my teeth and thinking of the joy those two kids took on the ice. Their commitment reinforced mine. In fact, it formed 90 percent of the reason I was able to motivate myself on those mornings.

When I lost my vision, I felt like I lost a lot more than just eyesight. I thought I had also lost the power to do things for other people, as well as the power to do some things for myself. I think playing hockey, for me, represented a way to take back some level of control over my life. Skating, then skating fast; shooting, then hitting the net regularly; the hours of practice that led to me scoring some goals—that all felt good for a little bit. But then the sense of accomplishment in those individual achievements started to wear off. Who the hell cares if a middle-aged guy puts a puck in the net in a beer league in D.C. or even in a blind tournament in Toronto? As I pondered this question, and as I worked with more and more kids like Nate, Aiden, and Axel, it started to dawn on me: the real power over my own sense of self-worth hid within the experience of helping other blind people achieve their own "firsts"—first time on the ice, first game, first goal. I think I realized that life—like hockey—is a team sport, and I'd been playing at life mostly as an individual since I'd lost my vision. Once I realized this, the additional awareness that I took more pride in tying a pair of skates than scoring a goal came quickly. This was ironic, though, at least in terms of the timeline. At this exact moment when I began to have this new mantra, I also was pushing hard to become one of the better blind hockey players in North America. I would soon be selected for Team USA. Yet I almost simultaneously stopped caring about individual hockey accomplishments in 2017.

I think I always knew while I was playing hockey that because I started so late in life, having been 37 years old when I put on skates for the first time myself, that it didn't matter how hard I practiced or how much money I spent hiring NHL power skating coaches or buying the best equipment—a ceiling existed for my individual achievements in hockey. A part of me always understood that.

As I found and competed in blind hockey, I also found the altruistic part of myself. It has served me well in my business life since then, as well as in my desire to grow friendships and a family. Every hockey player I impacted along the way, every single individual who is still on the ice, still doing great things in hockey, still on their way up as a player, and even those who have stopped playing but have integrated their experiences from hockey into a fuller and richer life, all those accomplishments loom for me as way more meaningful in the grand scheme of things. It's the difference between playing the finite game of scores and competition and benchmarks and achievement versus playing the infinite game of helping others grow, a game that continues to give, to expand, to ripple outward exponentially. This didn't dawn on me first in the military or in business or in raising a family. It came to me first through helping others learn to play hockey. What you accomplish in life can only live on through others, especially after you can't do it yourself. Teaching others to play blind hockey lit that light bulb for me.

And it changed who I am as a person.

Now when I walk into my office at work, the first thing I think about is the knowledge I can put into the heads of my coworkers, knowledge of the sort they can carry forward and use for 20 or 30 more years, even if I can only use it for another 10 or 15. That's probably the most important lesson that hockey taught me: the measure of a person, and their impact, can only amount to something significant if it resonates and creates ongoing impact through others.

Chapter 14

PRIORITIES

I'd enjoyed a perfect skating "career," and it had come to the perfect ending at the perfect time in my life. I was ready for a new phase to begin.

As I stepped away from hockey in March 2019, leaving Team USA, I found I had space and energy to reevaluate my professional journey. I realized that while I had been committing myself so fully to hockey, it had come at the cost of really committing myself fully to my professional endeavors. I'd put my career on the back burner, and that was okay, for a time. Now I felt the urge, and had the room in my life, to again go hard on things other than hockey.

I took a deep look at where my career stood. With Cosain, I had a good year in 2018, made good money, and as 2019 started I had a lead on a really good contract to do top-secret work for the Defense Logistics Agency (DLA). However, I knew this would be the kind of contract where I would build a team and not get to see them every day.

Onc thing I had figured out along the way, in my journey through hockey, involved the importance of quality social interactions for my well-being. Certainly, I needed money in order to live. I needed it even more to do the sorts of things all over North America on my own dime that I had been enjoying as part of my blind hockey pursuits—both playing and helping support the growth of the sport. Travel is a more rewarding but also more expensive social interaction than walking down the street and hanging out at the park. In contrast, though, doing work that would be largely isolating, in a windowless high-security room or apart from the teams I built and fielded at such facilities, would be higher paying but much less gratifying. Compounding matters, I'd also just ended the relationship with that orthopedic nurse practitioner right around this same time. The combination of drawing down my hockey activities, considering a big but isolating contract with the DLA, and ending this relationship really left me desperately seeking social interactions.

The sense of isolation, both physically and mentally, increased over the summer of 2019. I started to go out to bars with friends on weeknights, attempting to compensate for the sudden lack of social interactions at work or through hockey. I didn't have another Try Blind Hockey event lined up, either. I'd been riding the high from successful events in Philly and Raleigh. But I knew that too would soon wear off.

Government contracting didn't seem to be bubbling up any near-term work prospects that would help me spend more time immersed in quality work socialization.

Fetching about for a solution, and also because I found myself newly single that summer, I started dating like crazy.

Now, if you're a blind guy, dating presents some interesting challenges. Trying to size up a potentially interesting person from behind and from a few feet away, I've got to be even more careful—it'll often turn out to be a dude with just really nice hair.

That summer of 2019 when I started dating again, I knew there were beautiful people all around me in D.C., but damned if I could spot them. Especially not as quickly as the normal male, with finely honed senses allowing him to appreciate the subtle indicators of beauty in a face, in a smile, in the shape of a woman's body.

Yet I have had the privilege of being born in a very helpful era for a blind man intent on finding a partner.

Apps are a lifesaver.

That summer in D.C., I created profiles on at least three different dating platforms: Hinge, Bumble, and OkCupid. Although I've lost most of my eyesight, I can still hold my phone up an inch and a half from the better of my two eyes and get a nice close look at a potential date. It's awkward, sure. But I can do it in the privacy of my own home, and it definitely beats the alternatives: not knowing whether I'm hitting on a supermodel or a man with nice hair. Or, even more awkwardly, trying to stare from one and a half inches away at the face of a random woman after walking up to her in a bar!

I found that these dating apps at least partially filled the void hockey had left.

By the time I met Jenny in December 2019, I had put a ton of work into figuring out what I needed in a long-term partner. I learned that I didn't want to be in a high-conflict, high-drama relationship, and seeking out someone even-keeled who was looking for a true partner had become more important to me. I went on at least one first date per week that whole summer and fall after my prior relationship ended. I had stayed in that relationship because I was afraid that no good partner would ever want someone like me, blind and essentially a liability.

By the end of the year, I had begun negotiating to do what I really wanted to do: spend my days around people, rather than alone, having found a promising position in Baton Rouge, Louisiana. I was willing to leave behind hockey altogether. I was willing to leave behind the house I owned by renting it out. And I was even willing to close down Cosain, if it came to it, to immerse myself in a regular day-to-day schedule surrounded by bright people who could engage my mind. Cosain, and government contracting work more generally, just didn't seem to be providing opportunities to build the social work environment I craved. I could make money with Cosain, but I couldn't find a day-to-day situation that would really, deeply fulfill me.

Yet no sooner did I shift toward lining up this contract in Baton Rouge that my long hours, days, and months on the dating apps finally paid off.

At first, swiping casually right and left, I froze on her profile, thinking it must have been a joke, or a bot. I'd matched with someone clearly too good for me. Too good to be a mortal human, really. My first thoughts in trying to start a conversation were simply to test whether she was real, to see how long the dreaded "bot" of the dating app biosphere could hold a conversation before trying to get me to sign up to one paywalled site or another. As a blind person, I'm easily catfished. If a woman has posted a picture from 12 years ago, if she's lost all her teeth, checked in and out of rehab clinics, or is 50 pounds overweight, I can't really tell. That's just an added layer to the normal issues a man has when dating, especially when you're in your forties. Matching with a very attractive woman over dating apps, you're safest to begin by assuming a few things:

1. A hundred other guys are probably after her, so there'll be a low probability the interaction will lead to anything.
2. Some women, at least in D.C., seem to really be after money, especially if they're more than ordinarily attractive.
3. If she's that attractive and on the apps, then there must be something wrong with her.

4. She may not be real (and for me, and other blind men, the odds of her not looking like her profile photos also greatly increase).

Putting aside all these possible pitfalls, I introduced myself to this woman, whose name was Jenny. And as part of that introduction, I told her I was a hockey player. I was still playing in a Saturday night beer league, even if I'd put Team USA behind me. On our first date—and this just goes to show how much I didn't think our interaction would lead to anything, convinced that she was just *way* out of my league—I took her to a dive bar.

She showed up having googled me. She'd found all the clips about my hockey career. By this point I'd been featured on NHL Network. Many stories had appeared in newspapers, the *Washington Post* even, and in general a lot of content existed online, though I'd never had a first date research it so deeply before. But Jenny was playing for keeps with dating. And she's thorough.

Normally on first dates—and remember, I'd gotten this down to a science!—I refrained from telling a woman about my visual impairment until I decided I liked her. In support of this ruse, I would pick a place I knew like the back of my hand. That way I wouldn't need to bring a cane, and I wouldn't run the risk of bumping into anything, giving away my blindness before I was ready to discuss it. I'd also always arrive first so that I didn't need to look around for my date. They'd have to look for me and find me instead. I did this for every date, and I didn't change up my routine for Jenny.

The dive bar I chose was a place called the Tune Inn, which anyone familiar with D.C. will recognize as the oldest, dingiest hole in the District, a favorite haunt of retired firefighters. There, I seated myself in an inconspicuous booth and bided my time until she arrived, not nervous because I had such low expectations.

I can notice certain features about a woman. Different things stand out to me in greater magnitude than they stand out to most men. Most men focus on outward signs of beauty. I can't really discern most of those details. The things I can make out, especially in a public setting, are height, weight, and her hair—the length, and whether it's light or dark. That's about all I get from the visual cues. That's about all I get, looks-wise. Because of this, though, the physical sussing out ends quickly for me. I find a woman attractive or not. Then we move on to more important stuff.

Jenny walked into the Tune Inn—I later discovered—expecting to identify me by looking for my guide dog, or at least for a blind cane. She'd googled me, after all. She already knew I was blind, and she was the only woman I'd ever had show up to a first date forewarned. I felt in other dating interactions that I began with a massive strike against me: my visual impairment. I can't drive. There's a chance, since I'm the carrier of a genetic condition, that I might pass it to kids. I had no idea that this beautiful and super sharp woman walked into our first date already knowing about my disability, already accepting it. She knew, but I didn't know that she knew.

I was able to just relax and be myself.

I didn't hide my blindness for long though. It came out in the conversation. And, of conversation, there was plenty! Our first date lasted seven hours. By hour five, she brought the subject up—saying, "So, how do you not have a guide dog or blind cane?"

This just floored me.

Of course, she must have noticed when we went to the jukebox. I asked her to pick the songs, handing her money and playing it off as just being generous. But she knew what I was doing.

We talked about all the really important things in life: that we both wanted kids, that neither of us wanted to give up our professional lives when we had kids. We talked about where we wanted to live, and that we'd both been raised by single mothers. We'd both bought homes on Capitol Hill—six blocks from each other, no less—while we were with prior partners. And, as we found out throughout that night, we both enjoyed music, could handle our booze, and didn't want to let each other go home just yet—so we left the dive bar, went to a wine party, then dinner, then my favorite live music piano bar. We shared our first kiss while the pianist played "Georgia on My Mind" after Jenny told him about her home state.

I've only had one perfect first date since I lost my vision, and it was this one. Of course, I fell in love with her almost from the get-go. But the date itself was made even more special because she knew about my disability before arriving, still chose to come, and perhaps even found it endearing.

My only big regret about my visual impairment is that I can't appreciate exactly how beautiful the woman who became my wife is. I had a chance to date my fair share of beautiful women in my wilder single days, and some of that was fun—but I realized from my dating life that I value brains over beauty and character over style. Jenny has brains, beauty, character, and style—and I'm in the fortunate position that I don't have to choose from the above attributes.

We dated for a hot and heavy few weeks, beginning with that first date—December 13—and continuing right through the New Year. All my logic had gone out the window. I thought I had met the love of my life. We both said the "L" word to each other. I told her she was exactly what I was looking for. I also mentioned that I was in the middle of negotiating a contract in Louisiana.

Like I mentioned, I was still playing beer league hockey in December 2019, but right before meeting Jenny, I had completely torn my ACL in a pregame skate.

I didn't realize it at first. In fact, I played the whole game after injuring it. The ligament had already distended, like a worn-out rubber band, based on the stress my other surgeries put on it. During this game it simply fell out of its connection to my tibia. In the process it also screwed up the meniscus in my right knee. Before I left for Louisiana, I got it checked and decided to forgo surgery in favor of seeing if I could rehab it. One of the memories I have of the early dating period Jenny and I enjoyed is scooting myself up and down the stairs of my house on my butt because I couldn't walk.

So, when I think through the moments of reflection, sitting on the bench during some of my final games on the ice, tallying up all the injuries over the years, the ACL stands out clearly as the last of them all, the one that kind of made me think, *Okay, I'm going to Louisiana and leaving behind both hockey and this girl to whom I just pledged love, but I've got to get myself back around people. I've got to make a change in how I spend my days, in order to get my head right.*

That's more important than hockey, Craig, I told myself. *That's even more important than dating.*

I didn't quite comprehend at the time that, by leaving D.C. and taking some time for myself, I would really be putting myself through a "life partner finishing school." Yet that's exactly what I did. And it helped me emerge as the right person for Jenny. I didn't know it in January 2020. Back then, at the beginning of my Louisiana adventure, I simply thought I needed to go work in a social environment with invigorating people. I thought I had signed up only for a short-term contract. But the company in Baton Rouge quickly offered me a full-time position, making the separation from Jenny even more difficult, if not impossible. So I ended things with her. I think for a lot of leaders in sport, business, or any other field choosing a primary pursuit over love, or happiness in a relationship, seems like a binary choice. It felt that way for me at the time. Leaving Team USA, like ending my relationship with Jenny, felt like a sacrifice I had to make to take my life in the direction I wanted to go. The important difference I discovered was, I always knew I wouldn't play hockey forever, but I didn't know yet that I'd decide to spend the rest of my life with Jenny, and that I'd just dumped my future wife. I didn't know, when I headed to Louisiana, that I needed to shed hockey, shed the D.C. social life, and frankly shed dating as a whole for a while, in order to get right and realize what I really needed to prioritize in life.

Then COVID hit, while I was working in Louisiana.

The following months went by in a blur of work-from-home, of limited social interactions, and of living in a foreign culture, a foreign place in America. Rewarding work, for sure, but again isolating.

After six months of this, Jenny and I reconnected by accident. For the third time, almost in a Freudian-slip sort of way, I texted her by accident and she replied with some testiness: "Either stop texting me altogether, or let's have a real conversation."

I called her, simply to apologize.

We started talking again. And we didn't stop.

Even more amazing, I felt lighter as a human. Much of the emotional baggage that had made me want to get the hell out of D.C. and break the cycle I found myself in throughout the whole of 2019 had been unpacked. I was ready to commit. And that's exactly what I did.

I was working as the chief operating and technology officer of a $50 million company there in Louisiana. Yet trading that level of success ended up being easy when I started to think about and talk through the possibility of getting back together with Jenny. I made a professional decision that ended up being a good set-up for the most important of personal decisions—rekindling my relationship with Jenny.

I decided to bet everything on her that October of 2020, right during the height of the pandemic. I told her how I felt, and the next thing I knew she flew from D.C. to Baton Rouge to renew our connection. Together we drove back to D.C., arriving the night Joe Biden was elected president. Over the next 18 months, from November 6, 2020, until April 2022, Jenny and I went through an insurrection on Capitol Hill together; fled D.C., got engaged, and bought a house. I started a new job. We planned a wedding and got married in Vail, Colorado, during the week that Omicron spiked. Yet, throughout all of this, in the back of my mind, while my life was becoming extremely full and joyful, a small part of me felt like I had a little bit of unfinished business with hockey.

So a month after our wedding, in January 2022, I got back on the ice with the Washington Blind Hockey Club. This was the club formerly known as the Wheelers. Other people were now running the organization and had changed the name. After a few games I realized I could still play, two bad knees and all. Before each skating session, I now slapped braces on both of my knees. It worked, if only barely, allowing me to get back into rhythm.

I started participating in a few more Try Blind Hockey events again too. One of them led to a very special moment out in Denver, Colorado, while visiting Jenny's family there. I was helping a blind kid find a puck on the ice when the head of community development for the Colorado Avalanche, a man named Rui Encarnacio, leaned over the boards and called my name. He and two people from the Air Force Academy had come to show me a new electronic puck they had fabricated, perhaps something we could use in blind hockey. They'd been working with the Colorado blind team I'd helped start to put together an initiative to replace the heavy, expensive, ball-bearing-filled blind puck. This was awesome. I'd had nothing to do with it, but it was really cool to see my former university show up to an event with my favorite pro team and for Jenny to see both of these parts of the blind hockey world I had worked so hard to help develop: the enrollment of kids in the sport and the now-self-supporting effort to get these blind teams woven into the fabric of their communities, the blind game thriving, people coming up with new inventions and new ideas all on their own.

I decided during this time to go to Canada for one last try at the Courage Cup. As luck would have it, and as a perfect symmetrical end to my hockey career in Canada, I got drafted onto the team with both Jason Yuha and Mark Demontis. The coach played me as their linemate. We ripped through that entire tourney without losing a single game. I got my name on the Courage Cup for a second time, but I left Toronto like I'd committed a crime in Singapore and had been caned. My legs were covered from the top of my skates to the bottom of hockey pads with bruises and lacerations. I also felt a new sense of fulfillment to have gotten the chance to play competitive blind hockey with Jenny watching. She saw me in my power, even if in the waning days of it, and that was important to me—having her see this side of me that had been such a big part of my life for so long.

As I celebrated with my teammates in Toronto after hoisting the Cup, it kind of hit me: *Okay, I really have done everything significant in hockey that I can possibly do.*

So I rolled into Pittsburgh for our next tournament with the team already suspecting that it would be my last weekend of hockey. The final decision came to me on the morning of the deciding game in the competition. The previous day, I had served a penalty for tripping after taking a skater's legs out to prevent him from having a free shot at our goalie. His skate blade had missed my neck by millimeters. I knew intellectually that injury rates in hockey are less than eight per 1,000 athlete exposures. And I knew that both football and wrestling are much more dangerous than hockey. I was wearing a neck guard, which have been required in blind hockey since 2010. But for me, the choice was not to quit hockey because of fear, but to choose something that I'd always wanted to do and finally had the chance to do, which was create a family. The existential question I was really asking myself was not whether blind hockey was too dangerous for me to keep playing but whether the potential risks of continuing to play as a 45-year-old man outweighed the benefits of getting myself ready to play with a kid I hoped to have someday. As I sat in the penalty box, the near-miss replayed in my mind like a scene from the *Matrix*: a slo-mo, rotating, 360-degree replay, my life and all the goodness that had started to come from my relationship with Jenny flashing before my eyes. I woke up that following morning knowing it would be my final game, and I started informing my teammates before and during the game itself.

That brings our story full circle, back to my last shift in Pittsburgh. And I ended on a high.

Kevin Brown, now the president of the Washington Blind Hockey Club that I had founded, was on the team and was among those I'd told it would be my last game. He had found hockey, my blind team, when he was at a point in his life even lower than what I'd experienced. Through hockey, I'd helped him come back from that place in his life.

Now, he's there beside me on the bench, also playing defense. I'd agreed in that tournament to move back from my usual forward position to play defense in order to try and neutralize some of the other team's really skilled players, like Charlie Mitchell, Luke Miller, and Tony Chesrow, whose skate had almost clipped my neck. The hidden benefit of playing defense was that it gave me lots of time next to Kevin on the bench.

This is the eighth game I've played in the past ten days. Kevin looks at me. He knows I'm as out of gas as everyone else, but he tells me not to worry, not to think about it, and as the clock winds down to one minute, he says, "Craig, take my shift. Go out there and score a fucking goal."

So that's what I did.

And it was the perfect goal.

I've got it on video, which, admittedly, doesn't help me much, except as a means to provide proof to those with eyesight! For me, this mostly exists in my heart and in my memory, clear as day.

Aiden McCown, playing defense, chips the puck past one of our opponents, using the boards to deflect it back out onto the ice. One of our players, Timmy Caputo, scoops the puck up and takes two strides into the neutral zone toward the center of the rink. He dishes the puck over to me, successfully bypassing the last of the defenders. I find myself in a pack of two or three other skaters, but just enough in front of them that, as I crash toward the opponent's net, coming in along the boards, I take a shot.

It isn't the best shot ever made in hockey. It's not some huge wind-up or fancy flick of the wrist.

But that doesn't matter.

I don't hesitate.

The puck leaves my stick, flat, moving fast, and it finds the back of the net, sneaking under the goalie's shin pad.

I leave the ice on a high note and, as a way to cement my decision and mark the occasion, I begin to give away my gear, one piece at a time.

Things that were special to me—my Air Force Academy breezers; my red-white-and-blue gloves from Team USA—and things that just had some value to them still, like a new set of sticks, I made sure I found new owners who would not only appreciate them but also use them as they pursued their own dreams and goals in blind hockey.

With the possibility of having kids now much more present in my mind, I kept my skates and helmet, thinking I could envision a future where I might someday step on the ice again to teach my own son or daughter. That future would arrive two years later with the birth of my son, Pace. All in all, it became a much smaller and lighter load than the full bag of hockey gear had been. In fact, I double-bagged my remaining gear in two white plastic garbage bags just so that I could even give away the oversized hockey duffel bag that had held my gear throughout all this wild and amazing adventure.

The double-bagged garbage bag was what I held in my hands when I limped into the brunch, back in D.C., where Jenny sat with some of her girlfriends. She saw me and instantly knew: it wasn't just skates and a helmet bulging in the plastic bag; it was half of my lifetime dedicated to helping others, pushing my own boundaries, striving to make something excellent of a life that others might find limiting. I had contracted Stargardt disease through some quirk of fate and genetics, but I had managed to metamorphose it into the fuel that allowed me to find and make the most of opportunities.

I felt not a single regret, not in my heart, not in my mind, certainly not in my surgically repaired knees or ankles. I'd enjoyed a perfect skating "career," and it had come to the perfect ending at the perfect time in my life. I was ready for a new phase to begin.

Shortly after my son, Pace, was born, Jenny and I decided that it was time for me to rejoin forces with my longtime mentor and former boss, Srini Chennamaraja, at Akira Technologies. Srini is a wonderful man and a great dad, and as luck would have it, he was really looking to pivot Akira into the emerging technology space, with a focus on AI and Quantum. Akira welcomed me back as the chief innovation officer in July 2024, with one big change: I'll no longer need to air out sweaty hockey gear in my office after a mid-afternoon practice.

As I think about that period of my life, of playing and helping grow blind hockey, a few hopes cross my mind.

I hope another American gets his or her name on the Courage Cup three times and passes me in that honor.

I hope that Team USA eventually breaks through and beats Team Canada.

I hope that blind hockey becomes a Paralympic sport and, if it does, I hope I get to take my son to go see the first game. I'll be sure, then, to point at the players on the ice and say, "Your dad used to do that." And I hope that some of the skaters on that team just happen to have been among those 300-plus blind people for whom I helped provide the initial opportunities to get involved in the sport.

I hope somebody eventually breaks the record we set, me and all the volunteers with the Washington Wheelers, in getting those 73 people to show up at our very first Try Blind Hockey event. I want this because it would signal the sport as having become so popular that blind people from all around have started showing up. Organizers in the future won't have to beg them to come, like we did.

And, for the love of God, I hope my own son never has to play blind hockey. But if his luck is no better than mine, then I hope he plays the game even better than I have done.

ACKNOWLEDGMENTS

THIS BOOK IS ABOUT THE FIRST half of my life, and how the sport of hockey taught me how to play on the most important team I'll ever be on: the team with my wife, Jenny. You are the most important person in my life, and the core of that team.

I have many people to thank—both in doing the things that led to many of the events in this book's story, as well as in writing, editing, and finishing this work.

To my developmental editor, Will Buchholz: thanks for your faith in my story. You brought these words to life, and this book only exists because I put my story in your capable hands.

To my developmental editor, Will Buchholz: thanks for your faith in my story. You brought these words to life, and this book only exists because I put my story in your capable hands.

To Vladen Chase, the host of the *Never Far from Home* hockey podcast: thanks for advising me on how to tell this story, and for supporting this effort.

To my blind hockey family: Matt Morrow, Mark DeMontis, Doug Goist, Nick Albicocco, Kevin Shanley, Christine Calleghy, Doris Donley, Kelly Serbu, Tina Butera, Kevin Brown, and all of the countless volunteers who showed up in D.C., Denver, Pittsburgh, Raleigh, Nashville, Philadelphia, and even Maine and Louisiana—you all made this story possible, and made my life better along the way.

To all the hockey and skating coaches who invested their time into turning a 37-year-old blind guy from South Carolina into a player on the U.S. Blind Hockey Team: thanks for investing in me. Especially Lyon Messier and Benny Kwon, Andy Calandro, and Duante' Abercrombie for the pre-dawn skates where I learned all the basic skills needed to become a hockey player. To Margaret Dalton, a great skating coach and a good friend: thanks for the countless rides to the rink; for joining my Saturday night league and playing right alongside me. To Wendy Marco, a phenomenal power skating coach and an inspirational human: thanks for your creativity in coaching someone who can't see where the hell he is skating and giving me the confidence to fly out there. To Dan Jablonic, who was the Hockey Director at Kettler Capitals Iceplex when I came knocking, asking to play in a beer league: thanks for caring more about giving me a chance to be part of the game than you cared about getting sued.

To my teammates from my first hockey team, the Rebels, especially Nate Cook, Jim Mangani, Chris Barron, Jimmy Goodwin, and Andy Ashcroft: thanks for countless rides to the rink, for cheering your asses off when I scored my first goal (and kindly informing me that the puck was in the net), for naming me assistant captain, and for giving me a chance to be a part of your team.

To my teammates on Team Black at the Caps' rink, especially Don Marlais, Ryan Ullman, Barrett Hildebrand, Eliott Segal, and Blaine Nibley: thanks for giving me a chance to spend my Saturday nights with you guys on the ice.

To my mentor and friend Nelson Howell: thanks for your support and guidance throughout this journey, brother, and thanks for letting me tell the "Flaming Lamborghini" story. You've taught me so much over the years, and I'm grateful to call you an honorary older brother.

To my Team USA teammates from that inaugural season in 2018: thanks for pushing me, lifting me up when I needed it, putting up with my shit, and continuing to support me as friends both during and after my time on the team. Especially Doug Goist, Tim Kane, Dirk Morgan, Anthony Chestow, Mike Straub, Blake Steinecke, and Kevin Brown. You all inspire me.

To the Monumental Sports and Washington Capitals organization, especially Pete Robinson and Beth Lenz: thanks so much for supporting my crazy idea to put more than 70 blind people on the ice at once and being with the Washington Blind Hockey Club every step of the way since.

To the amazingly generous team at Kroenke Sports and Entertainment and the Colorado Avalanche, especially Deb Dowling and Rui Encarnacio: thanks for one of the most thrilling days of my life, giving me Ball Arena (at that time the Pepsi Center) to help a bunch of blind people try hockey. I'm incredibly proud of the work you and the Colorado Visionaries have done to grow blind hockey in the region.

To the generous people at the Pittsburgh Penguins, Carolina Hurricanes, Philadelphia Flyers, Nashville Predators, Vegas Golden Knights, Minnesota Wild, and St. Louis Blues: thanks for the chance to work with and through you to put blind skaters on the ice.

To my friends at Dawg Nation, especially the Dawgfather himself, Marty Richardson: thanks for believing in and supporting blind hockey from the first event in Denver and helping grow the game.

Thanks to my mom, Robin, for being the loudest one in the stands at so many youth soccer games. To my dad, Joe (wherever your soul may be), for instilling in me a lifelong love of sport, and to my brothers, Brendan and Conor, for supporting every step of my journey in hockey. I love you all very much.

And to my son, Pace, who was born during the writing of this book: this story is for you. Mom and Dad love you very much. May you never play blind hockey.

ABOUT THE AUTHOR

Craig Fitzpatrick played forward for the U.S. Blind Hockey Team, competing across North America. He has helped found numerous blind hockey teams. Craig is a longtime Colorado Avalanche fan and trained in Colorado during his competitive hockey career.

He graduated from the U.S. Air Force Academy and served five years in the U.S. Air Force before being diagnosed with Stargardt disease, leading to his near complete blindness and 100 percent service-related disability. He is currently the chief innovation officer at Akira Technologies, an AI and cybersecurity technology company in Washington, D.C.

Craig holds a master's degree in public administration (Summa Cum Laude) from Saint Louis University. His charitable work focuses on serving as a senior technology fellow at the Center for Advanced Defense Studies, where he guides C4ADS' technology commercialization efforts.

He has worked with the National Hockey League to build charitable programs that expand access to the sport for disabled children across the United States and Canada, including programs with five NHL teams. Craig and his wife, Jenny, reside in Great Falls, Virginia, and welcomed their son, Pace, in February 2024.